Exquisite
Ribbon Accessories

BY YUKIKO OGURA

Quilters' Resource publications

This edition first published in 1997 for Quilters' Resource Inc.
P.O. Box 148850
Chicago, IL 60614
tel. 773-278-5695
fax 773-278-1348

Distributed in Australia by
Sally Milner Pty Ltd.
RMB 54 Burra Road
Burra Creek NSW 2620
tel. 06-236-3412
fax 06-236-3446

First published in Japan in 1995 by
Japan Broadcast Publishing (NHK Publishing)
Copyright ©1995 Japan Broadcast Publishing (NHK Publishing)

Art Direction / Gohji Morofuji
Book Design / Yasuko Maruo
Photography / Masayuki Tsutsui
Styling / Yoko Watanabe
Co-Editor / Toshiko Hirakawa
Tracing / Minako Tsukabe
Editor / Mamiko Shibasaki
Hats provided by Boutique Salon Coco

English language edition:
Translator / Jennifer Ito
Editor / Marita Seaberg
Cover and Title Page Design / Darren Ching

ISBN 0-9629056-9-0
UPC 8750

PUBLISHER'S NOTE   When adjusting from metric to the imperial
system measurements have been rounded up and down when necessary
to help the reader.

C O N T E N T S

Most projects feature MOKUBA ribbon.
MOKUBA CO., LTD.
4-16-8 Kuramae, Taito-ku, Tokyo 111, Japan
tel. 03-3864-7700 fax 03-3864-4013
For ribbons, please contact Quilters' Resource
P.O. Box 148850, Chicago, IL 60614
tel. 773-278-5695 fax. 773-278-1348

Small Flower Purses

Combine your favorite ribbon colors and flower patterns to create an assortment of ribbon purses. (See page 58)

Spring Bouquets

Inspired by the spring season, these ribbon flowers are ideal for hair accessories and corsages. (See page 60)

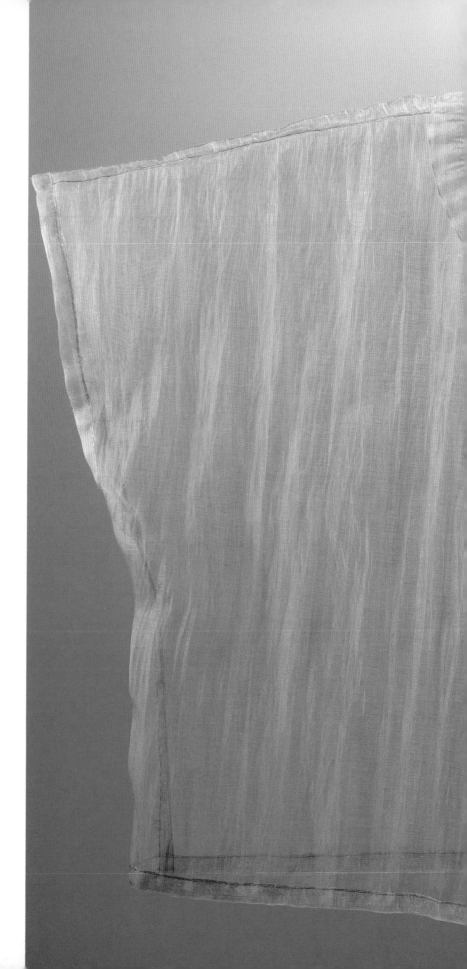

Organdy Bolero

Sheer and delicate, this organdy bolero transforms an outfit from casual to sophisticated. (See page 61)

Evening Hats

Elegant roses in a cage of veiling perfect for wedding attendants. (See page 62)

Antique Rose Purse

Recreate old-world charm with an antique rose purse made entirely of ribbon. (See page 62)

Framed Roses and Mini-boxes

A small frame overflows with elegance when filled with roses. The mini-boxes are made entirely of ribbon. (See page 64)

Linked Flower Hat Band

Tiny flowers are easily held together by threading a ribbon through them. (See page 70)

Peony Hat Ornament

This corsage adds a dash of elegance to a hat with a graceful silhouette. (See page 70)

Accessories in Muted Colors

Ribbon in muted autumn hues make classic corsages and hair accessories. (See page 66)

Ribbon Patchwork Bags

Velvet ribbons sewn together like patchwork and embroidered create charming, colorful bags. (See page 68)

Elegant Wine Hat Ornament

For a truly elegant look, match ribbon band and flower to your hat. (See page 70)

Velvet Rose Hat Band

A hat you've had for years becomes radiant when you add a charming decoration. (See page 70)

Accessories in Rich Colors

Combining textures in deep jewel tones creates the perfect accessory for suits and formal wear. (See page 71)

Drawstring Bags

Coordinating ribbon materials and colors is challenging, though the result looks simple and effortless. (See page 72)

Linked Flower Purses

This pentagon-shaped purse highlights the sharp edges of the folded ribbon.
(See page 74)

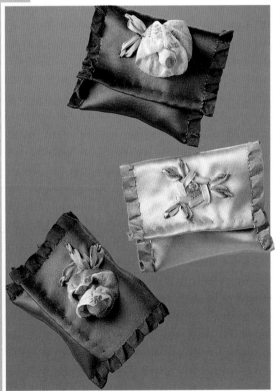

Small pouches are perfect for keeping special treasures like rings and earrings.
(See page 75)

Wedding Bouquet

A light and transparent bridal bouquet of rolled ribbon roses will be treasured. With matching gloves. (See page 76)

Embroidered Rose Pouches

Leftover wide ribbon is ideal for small pouches. The velvet pouch is for holding eyeglasses. (See page 78)

Black Satin Evening Bag

The contrast of satin and suede textures creates the understated elegance of this evening bag. (See page 77)

Assembly Techniques

In this book, many of the instructions for
assembling the flowers are new designs.
Please try making your own favorite
flowers by freely combining
these components.

Ribbons
Used Most Often in This Book with the Mokuba Style Numbers

No. 1150 Single-Face Satin
Ribbon

No. 1000 Rayon Satin
Ribbon

No. 1600 Picot Edge Satin
Ribbon

No. 0492 Pleated Satin
Ribbon

No. 0497 Ruffled Satin
Ribbon

No. 0488 Pleated Satin
Ribbon

No. 4895 Ruffled Edge
Satin Ribbon

No. 4512 Ruffled Organdy
Ribbon

No. 4546 Crepe Georgette
Ribbon

No. 4647 Pleated Crepe
Georgette Ribbon

No. 4499 Stripe Organdy
Ribbon

No. 4570 Metallic Edge
Organdy Ribbon

No. 4490 Picot Edge
Organdy Ribbon

No. 4615 Ruffled Edge
Organdy Ribbon

No. 4584 Textured Organdy
Ribbon

No. 4495 Taffeta Ribbon

No. 4522 Picot Edge Taffeta
Ribbon

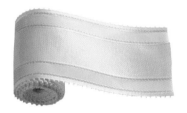

No. 4552 Picot Edge Fancy
Ribbon

No. 4876 Woven Check
Ribbon

No. 4643 Double-faced Velvet with
Satin Edge Ribbon

No. 2000 Picot Edge Velvet
Ribbon

No. 0500 Pleated Velvet
Ribbon

No. 4524 Check Velvet
Ribbon

No. 3272 Romantic Lace
Ribbon

No. 3124 Scallop Edge
Lace Ribbon

Making the Components

*Dark colored thread is used in the assembly photos for clarity. In actual projects use thread that matches the ribbon color. Use #8 Pearl Cotton or cotton embroidery thread for stitching gathers and attaching metal parts. (For more details see page 57)

GATHERING

Gathered Flowers (circle)

Simply gather the ribbon into a circle to make this flower. Just changing the color and texture of the ribbon, using two or three ribbons stitched together, or folding the ribbon in half and stitching can make a variety of different flowers.

Full-size templates for use with Gathered Flowers

*Use woven fabric or thick craft paper to make templates.

1 To shape the ribbon into a circle, loosely baste along one edge, then pull the thread to draw it up into a gather. An irregular gather looks more like a flower.

2 Stitch ends of ribbon together to finish seam. Tie off the end of the thread, and it's done.

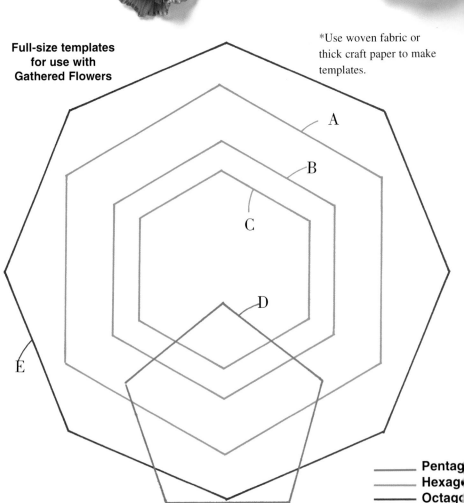

A

B

C

D

E

Pentag
Hexag
Octag

Gathered Flowers (polygons)

Fold the ribbon into a triangle, square, pentagon, hexagon, or octagon and gather to make three, four, five, six, and eight petal flowers. For polygons with five or more sides, use the templates to fold the ribbon into shape. Varying the width of the ribbon and the size of the template will create different petals on your flowers. You can also create a variety of looks by altering the fabric and style of ribbon and by using two or three ribbons together. When combined with other components, this flower can also serve as a foundation to make a larger flower.

◆Gathered Flower (square)

 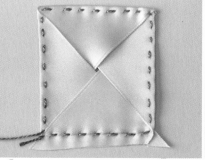 

1 Fold the ribbon back under itself three times and after the last fold place the end of the ribbon on top of the starting end of the ribbon.

2 Arrange the ribbon into a square, and draw a line across the overlapping ends to make a square. Then loosely baste along the edges of the ribbon only. Trim the edge where the ends overlap.

3 Draw up the thread, tie off and the flower is finished.

◆Gathered Flower (triangle)

1 Fold the ribbon back under itself two times, leaving a triangle-shaped opening in the middle. Loosely baste along the edges of the ribbon only, following the method used for the square.

2 Draw up the thread, tie off and the flower is finished.

*The shape of the flower will change depending on the size of the opening (square/triangle) in the middle. The larger the opening, the more the petals will open. If you make no opening in the middle, it will form the shape of a bud. In addition, depending on the sizes of the templates used for pentagons, hexagons, etc., the flower will open differently. Take care to use a template with sides that are no smaller than the width of the ribbon.

◆Gathered Flower (hexagon).....Follow these instructions for pentagons and other polygons

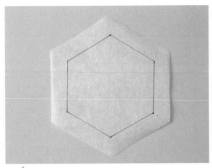

1 Draw a hexagon, then cut out the template, leaving an allowance on all sides that is about half the ribbon width.

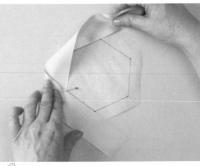

2 Fold the ribbon back under itself, matching it up with the lines of the hexagon and pinning into place as you go.

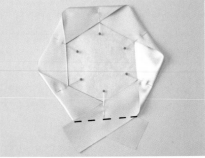

3 After folding the ribbon around all the sides of the hexagon, draw a line across the overlapping ends to complete.

4 Keeping the ribbon pinned to the template, loosely baste along the edges of the ribbon only. Trim the overlapping ends, leaving a small seam allowance.

5 Remove the template, then pull both ends of the thread at the same time to gather the ribbon.

6 To finish the flower, pull up the thread as far as possible, tie it off twice and cut. The six petals are turned in the same direction to make a pinwheel-like figure.

◆Gathered Flower (hexagon, alternating).....Also made with an octagon or any polygon with an even number of sides

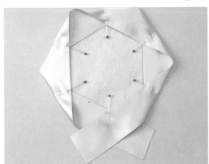

1 Following the lines of the hexagon, fold the ribbon alternately forward and over itself, then back and under itself, pinning into place. The ribbon will form alternating large and small triangles.

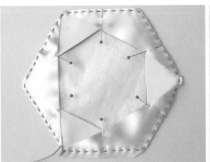

2 Keeping the ribbon pinned to the template, loosely baste along the edges of the ribbon only and trim the overlapping ends, leaving a seam allowance.

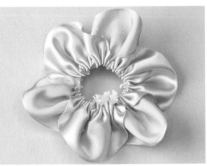

3 Remove the template, pull up the ends of the thread to gather and tie off. The upper three petals and the lower three petals are distinctly separated.

Rolled Rose A

A ribbon mysteriously transforms into a rose by simply rolling and stitching. Making a rose is easy if you use a pregathered or pleated (one-sided) ribbon. Depending on the number of rolls and the width of the ribbon, a variety of sizes can be made. You can also make sweet peas by changing the color and manner of rolling.

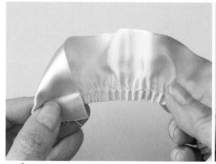

1 Fold the left end of the ribbon down into a triangle.

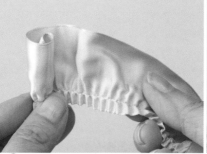

2 Starting at the left edge, roll the ribbon tightly 2-3 times to form the center of the rose.

3 Roll the ribbon around as many times as desired then fold it diagonally back.

4 Holding it at the base, wrap the ribbon around from the back to the front in order to circle the rolled section.

5 Cut off the end of the ribbon, leaving a small allowance. Fold the extra back into a triangle then stitch down tightly with needle and thread.

6 The finished rose.

Rolled Rose B

This rose, made by folding and rolling the ribbon, has the innocence of a fresh blossom. Its look changes with different types of ribbon and variations in the rolling method. Perfect for soft, transparent materials like organdy and chiffon. The photographs below show the ribbon being rolled from right to left, however, the same rose can be made rolling from left to right if you are left-handed.

1 Fold the right end of the ribbon downward to form a triangle.

2 Fold the triangle to the left toward the ribbon.

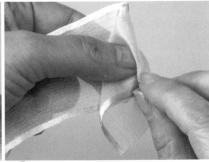

3 Make a pleat at the bottom of the folded section.

4 Roll the folded section once around the pleat.

5 Tack into place by stitching from front to back at the base of fold.

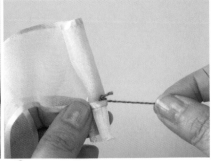

6 Bringing the thread around to the right-hand side, stitch once more from front to back, securing it tightly to form the center of the rose. Continue without tying off the thread.

7 Fold the ribbon backward into a triangle.

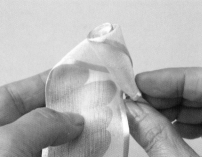

8 Roll the ribbon around the center section in your right hand, making the outside edge of the fold, from step 7, lie along the top of the flower.

9 Roll just past the end of the folded section from step 7 to the point where the rose petal is smooth, then fold the ribbon backward into a triangle again.

10 Repeat steps 7-9, taking care that the top of the ribbon is level and gathering together any extra at the bottom.

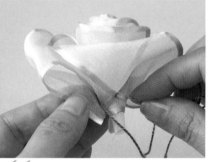

11 When you reach the desired size, fold the end down, and wrap the thread from step 6 around it 2 or 3 times. Stitch tightly into place.

12 Tie off the thread and cut. (underside shown)

13 The finished rose. Interestingly, each rose comes out differently depending on how tightly it is rolled. Try to bring to life a natural looking flower.

Rolled Rose C

The radiance of a flower in full bloom is created in this charming rose. The ribbon is stitched each time you roll it, but not too tightly, creating a softly formed, beautiful rose. Once you become skilled at making these, you can wait to stitch the entire rose at the end after finishing the rolling. From soft, sheer organdy to rich, thick velvet, any ribbon can be used. This rose can be made by rolling from the left end as well.

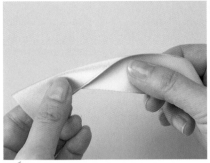

1 With the wrong side of the ribbon facing you, fold the end toward you and down diagonally.

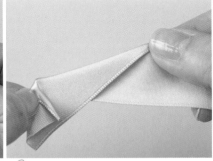

2 Slightly fold forward the end of the diagonal section again.

3 Roll it tightly once or twice to form the center.

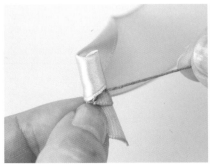

4 A small part of the folded section should remain. Tack the bottom edge tightly.

5 Twist the ribbon once to the outside and roll the twisted section around the center.

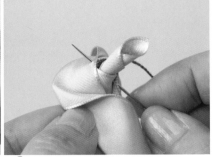

6 Turn over and tightly stitch together the rolled pieces from underneath.

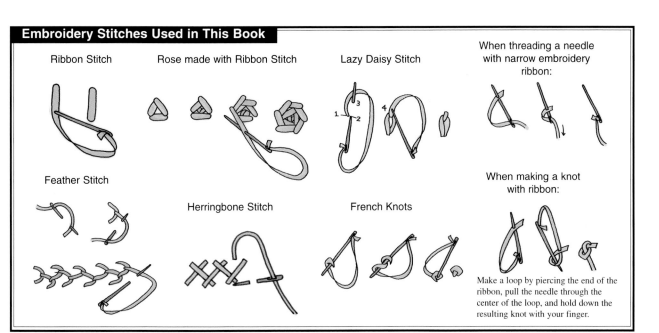

Ribbon Stitch

Rose made with Ribbon Stitch

Lazy Daisy Stitch

When threading a needle with narrow embroidery ribbon:

Feather Stitch

Herringbone Stitch

French Knots

When making a knot with ribbon:

Make a loop by piercing the end of the ribbon, pull the needle through the center of the loop, and hold down the resulting knot with your finger.

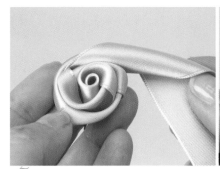

7 Continue twisting the ribbon and rolling so that from halfway around only the right side of the ribbon is showing.

8 With each round, turn the rose over and stitch together tightly from underneath.

9 Staggering the layers of the underside slightly with each round in order to make the top side level, stitch in place.

10 Repeat steps 8 and 9 until finished rolling, then fold the end of the ribbon in toward the center, stitching into place.

11 The finished rose.

Folded Rose

Made by folding Wire Edge ribbon (ribbon with thin wires running along the selvage edges) and stuffing with poly-fiber fill, this rose resembles a full bud that is half open.

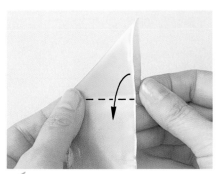

1 Fold the cut end of the ribbon back into a triangle, then fold the triangle forward and down.

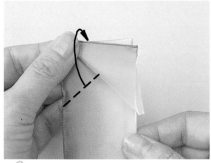

2 Being careful not to bend the triangle formed in step 1, fold the ribbon back again into a second triangle.

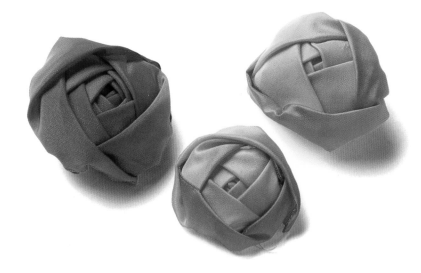

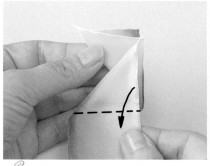

3 Fold the entire section forward and down.

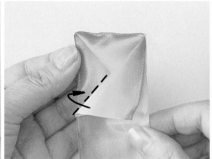

4 Fold the triangle section from step 3 again back diagonally.

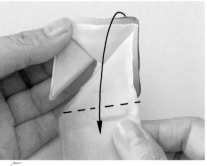

5 Fold the entire section forward and down.

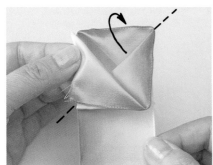

6 As in step 1, fold the section from step 5 back diagonally without bending the previously folded triangles.

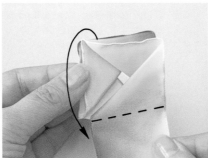

7 Again, fold the entire section forward and down.

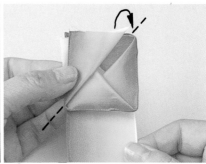

8 Fold the section from step 7 back diagonally. Continue folding triangles repeating steps 6 and 7. Match up the corners as much as possible.

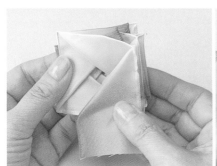

9 Fold the ribbon up to the end.

10 Turn the folded ribbon over and unfold the first triangle to cover the hole in the middle.

11 Turn back over to the top, and holding it with both hands push the center from the back with both index fingers, gradually loosening the ribbon to spread out the rose bud.

12 Once the bud opens, hold the outside edges of the flower in your left hand while pushing the center up from the back side with your right hand and arrange it into a flower-like shape.

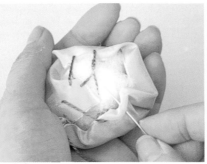

13 Stuff the middle with poly-fiber fill and stitch it together so that the flower will keep its shape.

14 The finished rose.

Folded Flower A

Alternating vertical and horizontal folded triangles create a star-shaped flower. This reversible flower can be used on either side.

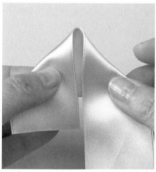

1 Fold the left side forward and down into a triangle, then fold the right side in the same way to form a peak.

2 Fold together the two triangles along the front center of the ribbon, then stitch together the two corners of the triangles.

3 Fold the long end of the ribbon up into a triangle to form a sideways peak.

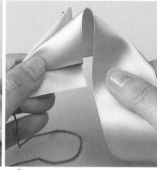

4 Fold the lower triangle up, then fold the long end of the ribbon forward and down into a triangle to form a peak as in step 1.

5 Repeat steps 2 through 4 until you have the desired number of petals, then matching up the beginning and end of the ribbon, sew the ends together.

6 Cut the ribbon along the edge of the seam from step 5 and tuck it into the triangle.

(front)

(back)

7 The finished flower.

Folded Flower B

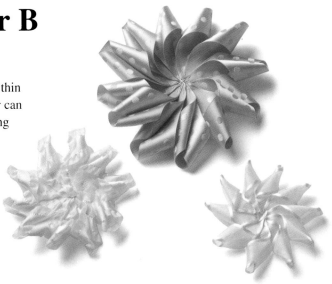

Make a full circle by folding long, thin petals out of ribbon. A large flower can be created by making the petals long and plentiful. The flower can also be left without sewing down the outside of the petals (as shown on the top flower in the photo to the right).

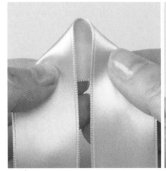

1 Measure a distance from the end of the ribbon that is about three times the ribbon width and fold both ends forward to form a peak.

2 Fold the right and left triangles formed in step 1 together along the front center of the ribbon.

3 Pin the fold in step 2 in place, then fold the long end of the ribbon up diagonally and form another peak as in step 1.

4 Pinning each fold in place, repeat steps 1 through 3 to make a circle.

5 Sew together the two edges of the folded ribbon in the center with one stitch. (Take care that the stitches show as little as possible on the front.)

6 Pull the thread back to the underside. Push the needle through just below the outer triangle at the edge of folded ribbon, sewing it into place with one stitch.

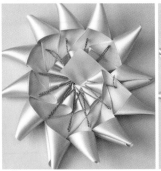

7 Repeat steps 5 and 6 using the same thread, sewing each petal into place in order. The thread will cross over the back side in a radiating pattern from the center to the outside.

8 The finished flower.

Loop Flower

This flower is made by weaving the ribbon through an embroidered hexagon. To make a larger flower, add more circles to the net. You can also weave into ready-made netting or net-like lace. Make the loop flower directly on a foundation fabric such as felt, then cut off the surrounding material for a corsage or a brooch.

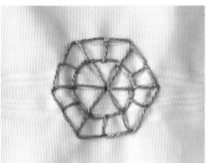

1 Embroider a hexagon on the foundation using a blanket stitch (shown in the picture below). Use a single strand of #5 Pearl Cotton.

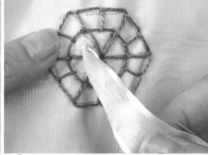

2 Thread the ribbon through the needle, and tie a knot in the end of the ribbon. Pull it through the base from back to front near the center.

3 Passing the eye of the needle through first, weave the ribbon over and back under one thread in the center tier of the foundation.

4 Pull the ribbon and fluff it into a loop. Pass the ribbon over and back under the next thread in the same manner.

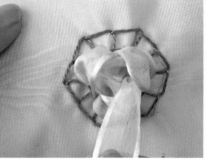

5 The ribbon has now been woven around all six threads of the inner circle. In the same manner, continue to weave the ribbon around the twelve threads of the outer hexagon.

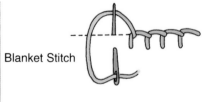

Blanket Stitch

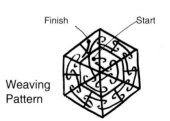

Finish   Start

Weaving Pattern

Leaf A

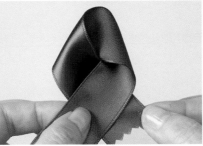

1 On the left end, fold forward a length of ribbon that is equal to about three times the width of the ribbon. Fold the right side of the ribbon back.

2 Cross the right end of the ribbon in front of the left end.

3 Cut off the excess ribbon, make a pleat at the bottom of the leaf and stitch into place.

Leaf B

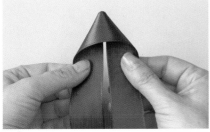

1 On the left end, fold back a length of ribbon equal to about four times the width of the ribbon. Fold the right end of the ribbon back in the same direction to form a peak.

2 Twist both the left and right ends of the ribbon towards the outside once.

Leaf C

3 Fold in half with right-sides facing in and pin in place.

4 Cut off the excess ribbon and stitch into place.

Fold in the same way as Folded Flower B, adjusting the number of folds to the number of leaves desired. After folding the desired number of leaves, stitch together in the fold.

Combinations

All the flowers introduced in this book are made by combining the flower elements that appear in the instruction section. Once you learn the methods for making the components, it's just a matter of putting them together. Choose freely from the many types of ribbons available. Combining colors, textures and sizes allows you to create an infinite number of different flowers. Bring to life flowers that reflect your unique sense of creativity.

Gathered Flower (square) + Gathered Flower (octagon)

Single Knot + Gathered Flower (circle with double fold) + Gathered Flower (alternating hexagon)

Single Knot + Gathered Flower (alternating hexagon with two ribbons)

Flower Assembly

After making all the components, put them together to check the look of the finished flower. Arrange the center piece with the piece that goes behind it and stitch them together on the underside in an inconspicuous place. Continue adding pieces one at a time from the center-top to the outside-back, stitching them together as you go. For flowers with leaves, attach the leaves last. When attaching the flower to a pin or a barrette, sew a small piece of felt on the backside over the places where the pieces are sewn together. (See page 56)

Single Knot + Gathered Flower (square) + Gathered Flower (pentagon)

Gathered Flower (square) + Gathered Flower (octagon) + Gathered Flower (circle)

Rolled Rose B + Gathered Flower (square) + Gathered Flower (octagon)

Rolled Rose C + Gathered Flower (pentagon)

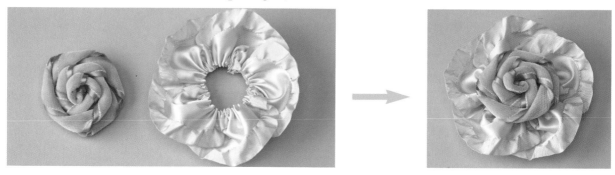

Folded Rose + Gathered Flower (square) + Leaf C

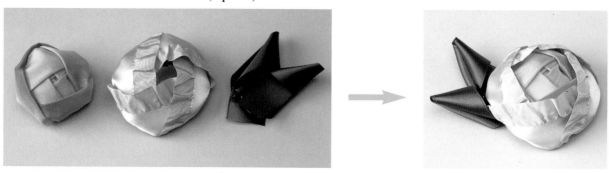

Single Knot + Gathered Flower (circle with two ribbons) + Folded Flower A

Single Knot + Gathered Flower (circle with two ribbons) + Gathered Flower (hexagon) + Folded Flower A (back)

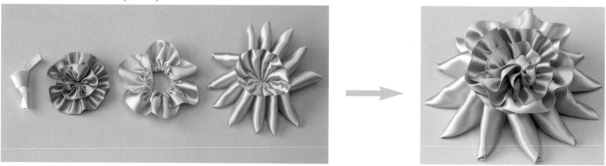

Single Knot + Gathered Flower (circle with two ribbons) + Folded Flower A (back)

Gathered Flower (triangle) + Folded Flower B + Leaf A

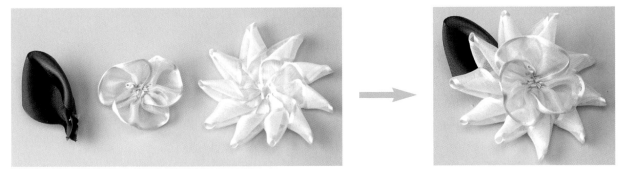

Rolled Rose B + Folded Flower A (back) + Folded Flower B

Gathered Flower (hexagon) + Threaded with Satin Ribbon

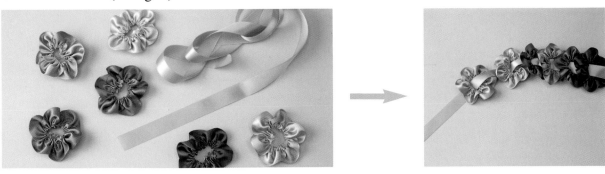

Attaching Pin Backs & Barrettes

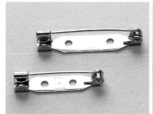

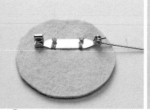

Pin Backs

1 Cut any excess ribbon and thread from the back of the completed flower.

2 Cut a piece of felt large enough to hide any stitches on the back of the flower. Attach the pin backs just above the center of the felt.

3 Stitch around the felt, attaching it to the flower. Use two or three strands of embroidery thread.

Barrettes

Attach the barrette slightly below the center of the felt. If the width of the barrette is longer than the felt, stitch the felt to the flower, then stitch another small piece of felt over the barrette, sandwiching the metal piece between the two pieces of felt.

Combs

Stitch the felt to the back of the flower, then tack down the comb toward the edge of the felt.

Hat Foundation

Combs and foundations come in many different sizes. Attach two combs to side of the foundation, one on the left and one on the right. (See page 62 for instructions)

Rolled Rose B Variation

Make Rolled Rose B, rolling to the middle of the ribbon.

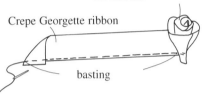

Crepe Georgette ribbon

basting

Pull the basting thread, gathering up the ribbon about halfway, then wrap around the rose and attach together.

Leaf C Variation

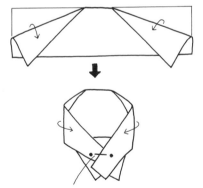

Stitch together.

Project Assembly Instructions

How to Use These Instruction Pages

● How to Read the Flower Assembly and Materials Chart

	Technique	Ribbon Type (Style #)	Width	Color (Color #)	Length
1	Rolled Rose A	Ruffled Satin (0497)	1in (25mm)	pink (65)	12in (30cm)

Order for attaching components together from the center to the outside.

• A star (★) in the column for ribbon width indicates that the ribbon is only available in one width.
• Most projects feature MOKUBA ribbon.

● Understanding the Materials Descriptions

The materials are shown in the following order.
Ribbon Type, Color, Length, Style Number, Width, Color Number.
   (ex.) Rayon Satin, pink, 12 1/2in (32cm) (#1000, 2in (48mm) col. 29)

• A star (★) for the ribbon width indicates that the ribbon is only available in one width.

● About Thread

   When making a Gathered Flower, different thread is used for basting, depending on the ribbon's width and thickness. For thicker ribbon, always use one strand of #5 Pearl Cotton, and for softer ribbon use three strands of embroidery thread. For ribbons made of thin materials like organdy, stitch with two strands of embroidery thread. Follow these guidelines to prevent basting threads from breaking when pulling them into a gather.

   In addition, when combining and attaching flowers together, use an embroidery thread in the same color as the flower so that it is inconspicuous.

Small Flower Purses

Instructions for Purse on Page 4   Finished Size: 7 1/2in (19cm) wide x 6 1/4in (16cm) deep

◆ Materials (excluding flower)

Foundation ......Pleated Satin, antique green,
 28in (70cm) (#0492, 4in
 (100mm) col. 15)

Ribbon for stitching.........
 Embroidery, antique green, 2
 1/3yds (200cm) (#1540, 1/8in
 (3.5mm) col. 366)

Shoulder strap ..Fashion cord, moss, 1 1/3yds
 (125cm) (#180, col. 18)

Other ....Matching #5 Pearl Cotton, matching fabric for lining, 14in
 x 8 1/2in (35cm x 22cm), one large snap

◆ Flower Assembly and Materials Chart

1	Rolled Rose B- Variation (see page 57)	Crepe Georgette (4546)	1in (25mm)	ecru (12)	28in (70cm)
2	Ribbon Bows (tie two ribbons together into a bow)	Pleated Satin (0492)	1/4in (6mm)	sage green (17)	16in (40cm)
		Cross Dyed Organdy (4563)	1in (25mm)	green (13)	16in (40cm)

Instructions for Purse on Page 5 (right)   Finished Size: 7 1/2in (19cm) wide x 6 1/4in (16cm) deep

◆ Materials (excluding flower)

Foundation ......Pleated Satin, cocoa, 28in
 (70cm) (#0492, 4in (100mm)
 col. 49)

Ribbon for stitching.......
 Embroidery, lt brown, 2 1/3yds
 (200cm) (#1540, 1/8in (3.5mm)
 col. 137)

Shoulder strap ..Fashion cord, ecru, 1 1/3yds
 (125cm) (#180, col. 12)

Other ....Matching #5 Pearl Cotton,
 matching fabric for lining, 14in x 8 1/2in (35cm x 22cm),
 one large snap

◆ Flower Assembly and Materials Chart

1	Rolled Rose B- Variation (see page 57)	Crepe Georgette (4546)	1in (25mm)	lt peach (64)	28in (70cm)
2	Ribbon Bows	Crepe Georgette (4546)	5/8in (15mm)	ecru (12)	16in (40cm)
		Pleated Satin (0492)	1/4in (6mm)	taupe (11)	16in (40cm)

◆ **Assembly Notes:** In Ribbon **2**, tie each of the ribbons into two separate bows, then attach together.

Instructions for Purse on Page 5 (left)   Finished Size: 7 1/2in (19cm) wide x 6 1/4in (16cm) deep

◆ Materials (excluding flower)

Foundation ......Pleated Satin, lt peach, 28in
 (70cm) (#0492, 4in (100mm)
 col. 64)

Ribbon for stitching.......
 Embroidery, pink, 2 1/3yds
 (200cm) (#1540, 1/8in (3.5
 mm) col. 102)

Shoulder strap ..Tube Satin, lt brown, 1 1/3 yds
 (125cm) (#4645, 3/8in (8mm)
 col. 45)

Other ....Matching #5 Pearl Cotton,
 matching fabric for lining, 14in
 x 8 1/2in (35cm x 22cm), one large snap

◆ Flower Assembly and Materials Chart

1	Gathered Flower (circle)	Pleated Crepe Georgette (4647)	2in (50mm)	lt peach (64)	8in (20cm)
2	Folded Flower B	Crepe Georgette (4546)	5/8in (15mm)	ecru (12)	1 1/3yds (125cm)
3	Ribbon Bows	Pleated Satin (0492)	1/4in (6mm)	cocoa (49)	12in (30cm)
		Tube Satin (4645)	1/4in (6mm)	cocoa (45)	12in (30cm)

Other: one pearl bead 1/4in (6mm) diameter, wire (thin) 12in (30cm).

◆ **Assembly Notes:** For Flower in Ribbon **1**, fold ribbon lengthwise and slightly off-center (do not line up edges) before sewing. For Tube Satin in Ribbon **3**, insert wire into center of ribbon, then bend as shown in the picture. Tie a bow in the Pleated Satin ribbon.

Purse Assembly Diagram

1. Cut the ribbon for the foundation into two 14in (35cm) lengths.

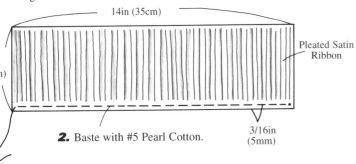

14in (35cm)

4in (10cm)

Pleated Satin Ribbon

2. Baste with #5 Pearl Cotton.

3/16in (5mm)

3. Pull up basting threads, gathering ribbon to finished length of 6 1/4in (16cm).

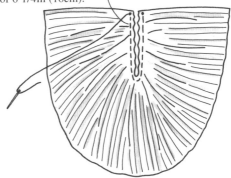

4. Fold in half, and whipstitch around the gathered section or stitch together with a blanket stitch.

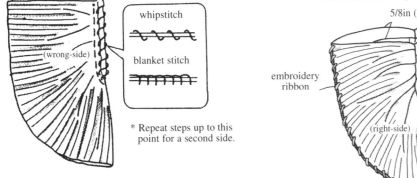

(wrong-side)

whipstitch

blanket stitch

* Repeat steps up to this point for a second side.

5. Fold in 5/8in (1.5cm) along the top opening edge of the purse.

5/8in (1.5cm)

embroidery ribbon

(right-side)

3/16in (5mm) whipstitch

6. Match both pieces, wrong-sides together, and whipstitch together around outside with embroidery ribbon.

7. Firmly attach the previously made ribbon bows and flower to the front of the purse over the center section.

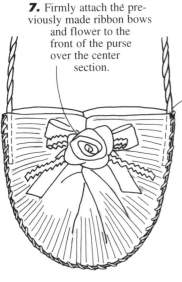

8. Attach the shoulder strap cord to the inside on both sides of the purse.

Stitch tightly into the folded-seam allowance.

(wrong-side)

9. Sew edges of lining together, put inside purse and hem around opening.

8 1/2in (22cm)

fold line

3/8in (8mm)   3/8in (8mm)

purse lining

fabric (wrong-side)

6 1/2in (17.5cm)

fold

cut

1 3/8in (3.5cm)

Stitch lining 3/16in (5mm) below outer edge of purse.

inner lining (right-side)

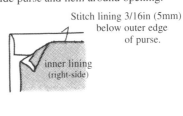

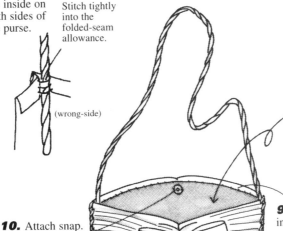

10. Attach snap.

How to Make Tube Satin Ribbon Bow for Purse on page 5 (left)

Insert wire in center of Tube Satin and bend.

*All three purses on page 5 and 6 can be made following these instructions.

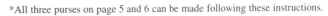

Spring Bouquets

Instructions for Flower A on Page 6

1	Rolled Rose A (make two roses)	Ruffled Satin (one-sided) (0497)	1in (25mm)	dusty rose (65)	6in x 2 (15cm)
	Rolled Rose A (make two roses)	Ruffled Satin (one-sided) (0497)	1in (25mm)	antique rose (29)	6in x 2 (15cm)
	Rolled Rose A (make two roses)	Ruffled Satin (one-sided) (0497)	1in (25mm)	lt peach (64)	6in x 2 (15cm)
2	Gathered Flower (hexagon)	Ruffled Satin (4996)	★ 2 1/2in (65mm)	beige (10)	25in (62cm)
3	Ribbon Bow	Metallic Organdy (4617)	1in (25mm)	cinnamon (9)	15 3/4in (40cm)

Other: matching #5 Pearl Cotton, felt (white) 2 1/2in x 2 1/2in (6cm x 6cm)

◆ **Assembly Notes:** Use Template A (hexagon) on page 38 for the Gathered Flower in Ribbon **2**.

Instructions for Flower B on Page 6

1	Rolled Rose B- Variation (p. 57)	Crepe Georgette (4546)	1in (25mm)	pale pink (31)	28in (70cm)
2	Gathered Flower (circle)	Ruffled Organdy (4512)	1 1/2in (40mm)	pale pink (31)	11in (28cm)
		Embroidery (1540)	1/8in (3.5mm)	pink (34)	1yd (100cm)
3	Gathered Flower (hexagon)	Bright Velvet (4480)	2in (50mm)	gray (5)	24in (60cm)
4	Ribbon Bow	Embroidery (1540)	★ 1/8in (3.5mm)	lt coral (52)	10in x 2 (25cm)

Other: matching #5 Pearl Cotton, felt (white) 2 1/2in x 2 1/2in (6cm x 6cm)

◆ **Assembly Notes:** Embroider Ruffled Organdy ribbon with French knots using embroidery ribbon, before making Gathered Flower in Ribbon **2**. Use Template A (hexagon) on page 38 for the Gathered Flower in Ribbon **3**. Tie together both pieces of Embroidery ribbon from **4** and attach between Flowers in Ribbon **1** and **2**.

Instructions for Flower C on Page 6

1	Rolled Rose B (make two roses)	Crepe Georgette (4546)	5/8in (15mm)	lt peach (64)	12in x 2 (30cm)
2	Gathered Flower (circle)	Romantic Lace Organdy (3272)	★ 1 1/4in (32mm)	white (2)	6in (15cm)
3	Gathered Flower (hexagon)	Ruffled Satin (4996)	★ 2 1/2in (65mm)	apricot (63)	24in (60cm)

Other: matching #5 Pearl Cotton, felt (white) 2 1/2in x 2 1/2in (6cm x 6cm)

◆ **Assembly Notes:** Use Template A (hexagon) on page 38 for the Gathered Flower in Ribbon **3**.

Instructions for Flower D on Page 7

1	Rolled Rose C	Silk Georgette (4472)	6in (150mm)	pale pink (31)	1yd (100cm)
2	Leaf C	Picot Edge Fancy (4552)	★ 2in (48mm)	beige (10)	20in (50cm)

Other: matching embroidery thread, felt (beige) 2in x 2in (5cm x 5cm)

◆ **Assembly Notes:** The ribbon for the Flower in Ribbon **1** is wide, so fold it in half lengthwise before using.

Instructions for Flower E on Page 7

1	Rolled Rose C	Crepe Georgette (4546)	1in (25mm)	lt peach (64)	20in (50cm)
2	Ribbon Bows (tie two bows)	Pleated Satin (0492)	1/4in (6mm)	lt peach (64)	14in (35cm)
		Single-Face Satin (1150)	3/8in (9mm)	lt peach (64)	16in (40cm) 4in (10cm)
3	Foundation	Pleated Satin (oblique) (0488)	2 1/4in (55mm)	lt peach (64)	12in (30cm)

Other: matching embroidery thread

◆ **Assembly Notes:** For the Foundation in Ribbon **3**, fold ribbon into a 4 1/2in (11cm) wide bow, wrap with 4in (10cm) length of Single-Face Satin, and tie around the middle. When attaching to a barrette or brooch, wrap around both Foundation and metal accessory.

Instructions for Flower F on Page 7

1	Rolled Rose B	Single-Face Satin (1150)	1in (25mm)	lt peach (64)	12in (30cm)
2	Gathered Flower (square)	Ruffled Satin (4996)	★ 2 1/2in (65mm)	apricot (63)	12in (30cm)
3	Gathered Flower (pentagon)	Ruffled Satin (4996)	★ 2 1/2in (65mm)	apricot (63)	20in (50cm)

Other: matching #5 Pearl Cotton, felt (white) 2 1/2in x 2 1/2in (6cm x 6cm)

◆ **Assembly Notes:** Use Template D (pentagon) on page 38 for the Gathered Flower in Ribbon **3**.

Instructions for Flower G on Page 7

1	Single Knot	Ruffled Organdy (4512)	3/4in (18mm)	pale pink (31)	5in (12cm)
2	Gathered Flower (circle)	Ruffled Satin (4996)	★ 2 1/2in (65mm)	dusty peach (40)	10in (24cm)
3	Gathered Flower (alternating hexagon)	Ruffled Satin (4996)	★ 2 1/2in (65mm)	dusty peach (40)	28in (64cm)

Other: matching #5 Pearl Cotton, felt (white) 2 3/4in x 2 3/4in (7cm x 7cm)

◆ **Assembly Notes:** Use Template A (hexagon) on page 38 for the Gathered Flower in Ribbon **3**.

Organdy Bolero

◆ Materials (excluding flower)

Fabric ....Crinkle Organdy, 1yd (90cm)
(#4467, 28in (70cm) col. 12)

Ribbon for binding....................
Organdy, beige, 3yds (270cm)
(#4563, 1in (25mm) col. 1)

Ribbon for neckline.................
Pleated Organdy, lt brown, 22in (55cm) (#4603, ★ 2 3/4in (70mm) col. 1)

Other ....A few seed beads, small hook and eye (one pair)

◆ Assembly Notes:

Cut out bolero pieces adding a 5/8in (1.5cm) seam allowance on shoulder and underarm seams. For other edges, do not leave a seam allowance, but cut out along finished-size lines. The bolero can be sewn by hand or by machine, but take care not to twist the ribbon. To sew by hand, use one strand of embroidery thread. Beads along the neckline can be attached after sewing the neckline ribbon in place.

Pattern

1. French seam the shoulder and side seams.

French seam

3. Fold Pleated ribbon in half over neckline edge. Attach beads every 3/8 in (1cm) while sewing ribbon in place.

4. Attach hook and eye.

5. Attach flowers.

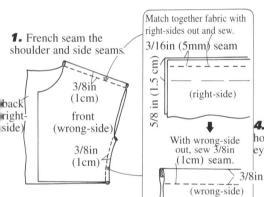

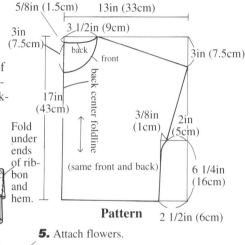

Bolero Assembly Diagram

2. Fold ribbon for binding in half around the edges of the fabric and sew with running stitch.

Fold under ribbon ends before stitching.

◆ Instructions for Flowers:

Make flowers 1-9 and attach to bolero with embroidery thread. The ribbon material is lightweight, so flowers need to be secured only at their centers.

[Ribbons Used]

Ribbon Type	Length	Style No.	Width	Color No.
Ribbon (a) Organdy (double edge)	22in (55cm)	#4584	★1 1/2in (38mm)	col. 94
Ribbon (b) Stripe Organdy	17 3/4in (45cm)	#4499	1 1/2in (38mm)	col. 64
Ribbon (c) Romantic Lace	2 1/2yds (224cm)	#3272	★1 1/4in (32mm)	col. 31
Ribbon (d) Romantic Lace	1yd (100cm)	#3264	★1 5/8in (43mm)	col. 40
Ribbon (e) Crepe Georgette	8 1/4in (21cm)	#4546	1in (25mm)	col. 64
Ribbon (f) Picot Organdy	14 1/2in (37cm)	#4616	★1 1/2in (40mm)	col. 40
Ribbon (g) Ruffled Edge	24in (58cm)	#4615	3/4in (20mm)	col. 64
Ribbon (h) Metallic	22in (54cm)	#4570	1in (25mm)	col. 9

[Instructions for Flowers 1-9] (Refer to page 38 for templates)

Flower 1 — Rolled Rose B, Ribbon (h), 12in (30cm) + Gathered Flower (hexagon template B), Ribbon (c), 16 1/2in (42cm)

Flower 2 — Gathered Flower (square), Ribbon (f), 8 1/4in (21cm) + Gathered Flower (octagon template E), Ribbon (a), 22in (55cm)

Flower 3 — Gathered Flower (square), Ribbon (c), 6 1/2in (17cm) + Gathered Flower (hexagon template B), Ribbon (b), 17 3/4in (45cm)

Flower 4 — Single Knot, Ribbon (h), 4 3/4in (12cm) + Gathered Flower (hexagon template A), Ribbon (d), 20in (50cm)

Flower 5 — Folded Flower A, Ribbon (g), 16 1/2in (42cm)

Flower 6 — Gathered Flower (triangle), Ribbon (e), 8 1/4in (21cm) + Gathered Flower (hexagon template B), Ribbon (c), 16 1/2in (42cm)

Flower 7 — Folded Flower A, Ribbon (c), 1 1/3yds (123cm)

Flower 8 — Gathered Flower with two ribbons (circle), Ribbons (g) and (f), 6 1/4in (16cm) each.

Flower 9 — Single Knot, Ribbon (h), 4 3/4in (12cm) + Gathered Flower, (hexagon template A), Ribbon (d) 20in (50cm)

Evening Hats

Instructions for Evening Hat on Page 10

◆ Flower Assembly and Materials Chart

1	Single Knot	Ruffled Organdy (4512)	3/4in (18mm)	pale pink (31)	4 3/4in (12cm) x 3
2	Gathered Flower (circle)	Pleated Crepe Georgette (4647)	2in (50mm)	antique rose (29)	8in (20cm) x 3
3	Gathered Flower (alternating hexagon)	Ruffled Satin (4996)	★ 2 1/2in (65mm)	dusty peach (40)	26in (64cm) x 3

Other: matching #5 Pearl Cotton, netting (black) 8in x 1yd (20cm x 100cm), one hat foundation (full size), two combs.

Instructions for Evening Hat on Page 11

◆ Flower Assembly and Materials Chart

1	Rolled Rose B (make three)	Crepe Georgette (4546)	1in (25mm)	antique rose (29)	1yd (100cm)
2	Gathered Flower (alternating hexagon)	Pleated Crepe Georgette (4647)	2in (50mm)	ecru (12)	22in (55cm)
3	Gathered Flower (octagon)	Ruffled Edge Satin (4895)	2 3/4in (72mm)	beige (10)	1yd (95cm)

Other: matching #5 Pearl Cotton, netting (black) 8in x 1yd (20cm x 100cm), one hat foundation (small size), two combs.

◆ **Assembly Notes:** Make three Rolled Roses from the 1yd (100cm) of Ribbon **1**. Varied sizes look the nicest. Use Template A (hexagon) on page 38 for Gathered Flower in Ribbon **2**. Use Template E (octagon) on page 38, enlarged 1 1/2 times (use a copy machine) for Gathered Flower in Ribbon **3**.

◆ **Assembly Notes:** For Gathered Flower in Ribbon **2**, fold ribbon in half lengthwise and slightly off-center (do not line up edges) before making flower. For Gathered Flower in Ribbon **3**, use Template A (hexagon) on page 38. Make three of each flower and attach to the hat foundation.

Attaching Combs

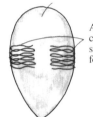

Foundation (wrong-side)

Attach one comb to each side of the hat foundation.

Assembly Diagram

1. Attach flowers to the front-side of the hat foundation.

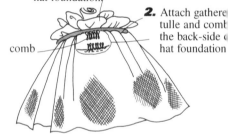

2. Attach gathered tulle and comb the back-side of hat foundation

comb

Antique Rose Purse

Instructions for Purse on Page 12 Finished Size: 7in (18cm) (diameter)

◆ Materials (excluding flower)

Foundation....................Pleated Satin, dusty rose, 1yd (100cm) (#0492, 3in (75mm) col. 65)

Facing for opening........Pleated Satin, dusty rose, 14 1/4in (36cm) (#0492, 1in (25mm) col. 65)

Flower linking ribbon...Pleated Satin, dusty rose, 32in (80cm) (#0492, 1/4in (6mm) col. 65)

Shoulder strap..............Tube Satin, pink, 1 1/3yds (120cm) (#4645, 1/4in (6mm) col. 94)

Embroidery ribbon ....Embroidery, pink, 3 1/3yds (300cm) (#1540, 1/8in (3.5mm) col. 34)

Other............................One skein embroidery thread, matching fabric for lining 24in x 8in (60cm x 20cm), two pearl beads, 1/4in (6mm) diameter, one large snap

◆ Instruction for Flowers

Make Flowers 1-10, then following the diagram below, secure the centers of the flowers to the purse using embroidery thread.

[Ribbons Used]

	Ribbon Type	Length	Style No.	Width	Color No.
Ribbon (a)	Pleated Satin	6in (15cm)	#0492	5/8in (15mm)	col. 31
Ribbon (b)	Pleated Satin	6in (15cm)	#0492	5/8in (15mm)	col. 64
Ribbon (c)	Ruffled Satin (one-sided)	34in (85cm)	#0497	1in (25mm)	col. 65
Ribbon (d)	Ruffled Satin (one-sided)	6in (15cm)	#0497	1in (25mm)	col. 64
Ribbon (e)	Ruffled Satin (one-sided)	6in (15cm)	#0497	1in (25mm)	col. 29
Ribbon (f)	Crepe Georgette	12in (30cm)	#4546	5/8in (15mm)	col. 12
Ribbon (g)	Pleated Georgette	30in (76cm)	#4647	2in (50mm)	col. 64
Ribbon (h)	Ruffled Organdy	6in (15cm)	#4512	1 1/2in (40mm)	col. 31

[Instructions for Flowers 1-10] (Refer to page 38 for templates)

Flower 1   Gathered Flower (circle), Ribbon (c), 6in (15cm)

Flower 2   Gathered Flower (circle), Ribbon (h), 6in (15cm) + Folded Flower A, Ribbon (c), 15 3/4in (40cm)

Flower 3   Gathered Flower (circle), Ribbon (g), 7 1/2in (19cm)

Flower 4   Gathered Flower (circle), Ribbon (c), 6in (15cm), Ribbon (f), 6in (15cm)

Flower 5   Gathered Flower (circle), Ribbon (g), 7 1/2in (19cm)

Flower 6   Gathered Flower (circle), Ribbon (e), 6in (15cm), Ribbon (f), 6in (15cm)

Flower 7   Gathered Flower (circle), Ribbon (g), 7 1/2in (19cm)

Flower 8   Gathered Flower (circle), Ribbon (b), 6in (15cm), Ribbon (d), 6in (15cm)

Flower 9   Gathered Flower (circle), Ribbon (g), 7 1/2in (19cm)

Flower 10 Gathered Flower (circle), Ribbon (a), 6in (15cm), Ribbon (c), 6in (15cm)

2. Baste along one edge of the ribbon and gather tightly.

1. Cut ribbon for Foundation into a 20in (50cm) length and sew together ends to form a circle.

3/8in (1cm)

3in (7.5cm)

(wrong-side)

Pleated Satin

3. Cut ribbon for facing of opening into 7in (18cm) lengths, place along edge of Foundation and whipstitch together with embroidery ribbon.

3/8in (1cm)

seam

(wrong-side)

*Repeat for second side.

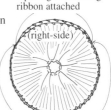

Opening with facing ribbon attached

(right-side)

4. Match sides, wrong sides together and whipstitch around outside with embroidery ribbon.

5. Attach assembled flowers.

<back>

beads

(right-side)

Attach Flower 1 to cover the hole in the center of the gather.

<front>

(right-side)

Attach Flower 2 to the center.

Thread 3 to 10 Flowers onto linking ribbon and attach to the front of purse in a circle, tying ends of ribbon in bow at top.

6. Make lining in the same way as the bag facing, using lining fabric.

Cut small circle of fabric to cover the center gather and stitch in place.

3/8in (1cm) seam allowance

(right-side)

Do not stitch together at opening of bag.

(wrong-side)

Sew 20in x 4in (50cm x 10cm) piece of fabric into a circle.

Match both panels with right-sides together and stitch, leaving top section over.

7. Attach the ribbon for the shoulder strap to the Foundation.

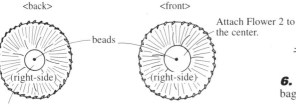

8. Tuck lining, wrong sides together, inside below the opening and hem.

9. Attach the snap.

Instructions for Flower on Page 13

◆ Flower Assembly and Materials Chart

1	Gathered Flower (square)	Pleated Crepe Georgette (4647)	2in (50mm)	lt peach (64)	12in (29cm)
2	Gathered Flower (octagon)	Pleated Crepe Georgette (4647)	2in (50mm)	lt peach (64)	26in (65cm)
3	Leaf A	Metallic Edge Organdy (4617)	1in (25mm)	green (6)	12in (30cm)

Other: matching #5 Pearl Cotton, felt (white) 2 1/2in x 2 1/2in (6cm x 6cm)

◆ **Assembly Notes:** For Gathered Flower in Ribbon **2**, use Template E (octagon) on page 38. For Leaf in Ribbon **3**, fold two leaves continuously with the same piece of ribbon, place the bases of the leaves together and stitch, then attach to the flower.

Framed Roses and Mini-boxes

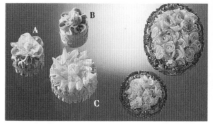

Instructions for Box A on Page 14 Finished Size: 2 3/4in (7cm) diameter x 2 1/2in (6cm) height

◆ Materials (excluding flowers)

Ribbon for covering box.................

    Ruffled Satin, dusty rose, 21in (52cm) (#0497, 2in (50mm) col. 65)

Box.................Diameter: 2 3/4in (70mm) height: 2 1/2in (60mm)

Other ....Matching #5 Pearl Cotton, small amount of poly-fiber fill, art board (dusty rose) 2 1/2in (6.5cm) diameter circle, double-sided tape

◆ Flower Assembly and Materials Chart

1	Gathered Flower (square)	Crepe Georgette (4546)	1in (25mm)	ecru (12)	6 1/4in (16cm)
2	Gathered Flower (hexagon)	Ruffled Organdy (4512)	1 1/2in (40mm)	pale pink (31)	15in (38cm)
3	Gathered Flower, with two ribbons together (hexagon)	Rayon Satin (1000)	1 1/2in (36mm)	antique rose (29)	20in (50cm)
		Woven Check (4876)	1 1/2in (36mm)	pale pink (31)	20in (50cm)

◆ **Assembly Notes:** Stuff the inside of Flower in Ribbon **1** with poly-fiber fill. For Flower in Ribbon **2**, use Template B (hexagon) on page 38. For Flower in Ribbon **3**, use Template A.

Instructions for Decorative Box B on Page 14 Finished Size: 2 3/4in (7cm) diameter x 2 1/2in (6cm) height

◆ Materials (excluding flowers)

Ribbon for covering box.................

    Jacquard, dusty peach, 21in (52cm) (#4851, 1 1/2in (36mm) col.40), Frill Tape, dusty peach, 21in (52cm) (#4571, col.40)

Box.................Diameter: 2 3/4in (70mm) height: 2 1/2in (60mm)

Other ....Matching #5 Pearl Cotton, small amount of poly-fiber fill, art board (dusty peach) 2 1/2in (6.5cm) diameter circle, double-sided tape

◆ Flower Assembly and Materials Chart

1	Two-sided Gather	Crepe Georgette (4546)	1 1/2in (38mm)	antique rose (29)	4 1/2in (11cm)
2	Gathered Flower (hexagon)	Rayon Satin (1000)	1in (25mm)	pale pink (31)	12in (31cm)
3	Gathered Flower (hexagon)	Rayon Satin (1000)	1 1/2in (36mm)	dusty peach (40)	16 1/2in (42cm)

◆ **Assembly Notes:** For Flower in Ribbon **1**, sew ribbon into a circle and baste, stitch along both edges. Stuff middle with poly-fiber fill and pull up basting threads. For Flower in Ribbon **2**, use Template C (hexagon) on page 38. Use Template B for Flower in Ribbon **3**. Place one piece of double-sided tape around the lid and the bottom of the box where they meet. Peel back paper on the tape and attach Jacquard ribbon. Attach a second piece of double-sided tape around lid and bottom of box where they meet. Attach narrow ruffled ribbon around the opening edge of box.

Instructions for Decorative Box C on Page 14 Finished Size: 4 1/2in (11cm) diameter x 2 1/4in (5.5cm) height

◆ Materials (excluding flowers)

Ribbon for covering box.................

    Ruffled Satin, ecru, 32in (80cm) (#0497, 2in (50mm) col.12)

Box.................Diameter: 4 1/2in (110mm) height: 2 1/4in (55mm)

Other ....Matching #5 Pearl Cotton, embroidery thread, art board (ecru) 4in (10cm) diameter circle, double-sided tape

◆ Flower Assembly and Materials Chart

1	Gathered Flower (square)	Textured Organdy (double edge) (4584)	★ 1 1/2in (38mm)	peach (94)	7in (18cm)
2	Gathered Flower (octagon)	Romantic Lace (Organdy) (3272)	★ 1 1/4in (32mm)	pale pink (31)	24in (60cm)
3	Folded Flower B	Crepe Georgette (4546)	1in (25mm)	lt peach (64)	2 1/3yds (200cm)

◆ **Assembly Notes:** For Gathered Flower in Ribbon **2**, use Template E (octagon) on page 38

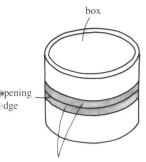

box

opening edge

1. Attach double-sided tape around each opening.

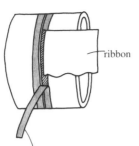

ribbon

2. Peel the paper backing from the double-sided tape, match the ribbon edge to the opening edge.

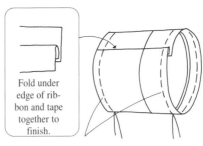

Fold under edge of ribbon and tape together to finish.

3. Baste stitch around outside edges of ribbon.

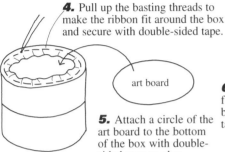

4. Pull up the basting threads to make the ribbon fit around the box and secure with double-sided tape.

art board

5. Attach a circle of the art board to the bottom of the box with double-sided tape or glue.

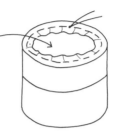

6. Attach assembled flower to the lid of the box with double-sided tape or glue.

Instructions for Decorative Frame (circle) on Page 15 — Finished Size: 3 1/2in (9cm) diameter

◆ **Materials**

Flowers......Crepe Georgette, ecru, 5yds (450cm) (#4546, 5/8in (15mm) col. 12)

Other ....Batting and fabric for foundation, 5in x 5in (13cm x 13cm) each, art board 3 1/2in x 3 1/2in (9cm x 9cm), matching embroidery thread, round frame with inside diameter of 3 1/2in (9cm)

◆ **Assembly Notes:** Make 21 to 22 of Rolled Rose B using approximately 8in of ribbon. Create a foundation by placing fabric on top of batting. Randomly stitch roses to foundation, keeping them in the 3 1/2in (9cm) open space of the frame.

Instructions for Decorative Frame (oval) on Page 15 — Finished Size: 5in (13cm) x 7in (17cm) (at the widest point)

◆ **Materials**

Flowers......Crepe Georgette, lt peach, 9 1/3yds (850cm) (#4546, 1in (25mm) col. 64)

Other ....Batting and fabric for foundation, 7in x 8 1/4in (17cm x 21cm) each, art board 5in x 7in (13cm x 17cm), matching embroidery thread, oval frame with inside diameter of 5in x 7in (13cm x 17cm)

◆ **Assembly Notes:** Make 28 Rolled Rose B using 12in (30cm) of ribbon for each rose. Create a foundation by placing fabric on top of batting. Randomly stitch roses to foundation, keeping them in an oval approximately 5in x 7in (13cm x 17cm).

1. Cut the art board to fit into the frame.

2. Place finished foundation on the art board and baste stitch around the fabric.

3. Pull up the basting threads to gather and tie off tightly.

4. Attach the previously assembled flowers to the foundation and insert it into the frame.

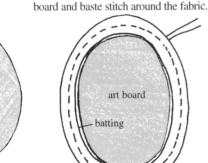

art board

art board

batting

Cut approximately 3/4in (2cm) larger.

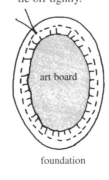

art board

foundation

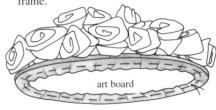

art board

Accessories in Muted Colors

Instructions for Flower A on Page 18

◆ Flower Assembly and Materials Chart

1	Rolled Rose C	Picot Edge Velvet (2000)	1 1/2in (36mm)	beige (11)	28in (70cm)
2	Leaf A (make two)	Picot Edge Fancy (4552)	★ 2in (47mm)	olive drab (59)	7in x 2 (18cm)

Other: matching embroidery thread, felt (white) 2 1/2in x 2 1/2in (6cm x 6cm)

Instructions for Flower B on Page 18

◆ Flower Assembly and Materials Chart

1	Gathered Flower (square)	Romantic Lace (Organdy) (3272)	★ 1 1/4in (32mm)	white (2)	6 1/2in (17cm)
2	Gathered Flower (circle)	Ruffled Organdy (4474)	1 3/8in (35mm)	pale pink (31)	7in (18cm)
3	Gathered Flower (alternating hexagon)	Pleated Crepe Georgette (4647)	2in (50mm)	antique green (15)	24in (60cm)

Other: matching embroidery thread, felt (beige) 1 5/8in x 1 5/8in (4cm x 4cm)

◆ **Assembly Notes:** Use Template A (hexagon) on page 38 for Gathered Flower in Ribbon **3**.

Instructions for Flower C on Page 18

◆ Flower Assembly and Materials Chart

1	Single Knot	Pleated Crepe Georgette (4647)	2in (50mm)	ecru (12)	6in (15cm)
2	Gathered Flower, with two ribbons (alternating hexagon)	Pleated Crepe Georgette (4647)	2in (50mm)	antique green (15)	24in (60cm)
		Stripe Organdy (4550)	★ 2in (50mm)	sage green (17)	24in (60cm)
3	Leaf C Variation	Picot Edge Fancy (4552)	★ 2in (48mm)	beige (10)	7in (18cm)

Other: matching #5 Pearl Cotton, felt (moss green) 2 1/2in x 2 1/2in (6cm x 6cm)

◆ **Assembly Notes:** For Flower in Ribbon **2**, place both ribbons together and fold. Use Template A (hexagon) on page 38. See page 57 for instructions for Leaf in Ribbon **3**.

Instructions for Flower D on Page 18

◆ Flower Assembly and Materials Chart

1	Folded Rose	Wire Edge (533)	1 1/2in (40mm)	pink (17)	1yd (100cm)
2	Gathered Flower (square)	Ruffled Satin (4996)	★ 2 1/2in (65mm)	beige (10)	15in (38cm)
3	Leaf A	Picot Edge Fancy (4552)	★ 2in (48mm)	olive drab (59)	16in (40cm)

Other: matching #5 Pearl Cotton, felt (black) 1 5/8in x 2 1/2in (4cm x 6cm), small amount of poly-fiber fill.

Instructions for Flower E on Page 19

◆ Flower Assembly and Materials Chart

1	Gathered Flower (square)	Single-Face Satin (1150)	1in (25mm)	a= (4) b= (49) c= (8)	6in (15cm) each
2	Gathered Flower (hexagon)	Single-Face Satin (1150)	1in (25mm)	a= (5) b= (15) c= (14)	12in (31cm) each
3	Ribbon Bow	Embroidery (1100)	1/8in (3.5mm)	(59) (48) (15)	20in (50cm) each

Other: matching #5 Pearl Cotton, felt (gray) 2 1/2in x 2 1/2in (6cm x 6cm)

◆ **Assembly Notes:** For each flower, make one for each of the three colors a, b, and c. Use Template C (hexagon) on page 38 for Flower in Ribbon **2**. For the Ribbon Bow in Ribbon **3**, fold all three ribbons in half together to make six, then fold in half again, stitching all the ends together. With the loops facing down, attach to a piece of felt. Cover by stitching three flowers on top. Trim away the excess felt.

Instructions for Flower F on Page 19

◆ Flower Assembly and Materials Chart

1	Gathered Flower (hexagon)	Single-Face Satin (1150)	1in (25mm)	beige (10)	12in (31cm) x 4
		Single-Face Satin (1150)	1in (25mm)	fawn (48)	12in (31cm)
		Single-Face Satin (1150)	1in (25mm)	cocoa (49)	12in (31cm)
		Single-Face Satin (1150)	1in (25mm)	chestnut (8)	12in (31cm)
2	Ribbon for Threading Flowers	Picot Edge Velvet (2000)	1in (24mm)	dark brown (7)	1yd (100cm)

Other: matching embroidery thread

◆ **Assembly Notes:** Use Template C (hexagon) on page 38 for Gathered Flowers in Ribbon **1**. Make seven flowers and thread with Ribbon **2** through the center holes. Arrange the flowers so that the seams do not show and stitch them in place.

Instructions for Flower G on Page 19

◆ Flower Assembly and Materials Chart

1	Rolled Rose C	Picot Edge Satin (1600)	1in (24mm)	beige (10)	24in (60cm)
2	Gathered Flower (hexagon)	Bright Velvet (4480)	2in (50mm)	beige (10)	24in (60cm)

Other: matching #5 Pearl Cotton, felt (beige) 2 3/4in x 2 3/4in (7cm x 7cm)

◆ **Assembly Notes:** Use Template A (hexagon) on page 38 for Gathered Flower in Ribbon **2**.

Instructions for Flower H on Page 19

◆ Flower Assembly and Materials Chart

1	Gathered Flower (square)	Single-Face Satin (1150)	1in (25mm)	tea (14)	6in (15cm)
2	Gathered Flower (alternating hexagon)	Single-Face Satin (1150)	1in (25mm)	antique green (15)	12in (31cm)
3	Gathered Flower (alternating hexagon)	Single-Face Satin (1150)	1 1/2in (36mm)	lt peach (64)	18in (45cm)

Other: matching #5 Pearl Cotton, felt (white) 2in x 2in (5cm x 5cm)

◆ **Assembly Notes:** Use Template C (hexagon) on page 38 for Gathered Flower in Ribbon **2**, and use Template B (hexagon) for Gathered Flower in Ribbon **3**.

Ribbon Patchwork Bags

Instructions for Bag on Page 20 Finished Size: 8 1/4in (21cm) x 8 1/4in (21cm) with 3/4in (2cm) gus

◆ Materials (excluding flowers)

Foundation ....All ribbon is Double-Faced Velvet (#4643)

(a) powder pink	6in (15cm)	(3in (75mm) col. 91)
(b) dusty rose	18in (44cm)	(1in (25mm) col. 65)
(c) pale blue	18in (44cm)	(1in (25mm) col. 44)
(d) pale lilac	24in (60cm)	(1in (25mm) col. 27)
(e) dk mauve	24in (60cm)	(1in (25mm) col. 92)
(f) pale lilac	32in (80cm)	(1 1/2in (36mm) col. 27)
(g) dk mauve	32in (80cm)	(1 1/2in (36mm) col. 92)

Facing for opening ..Picot Edge Velvet, gray, 18in (46cm) (#2000, 1in (24mm) col. 5)

Gusset and shoulder strap......................
     Picot Edge Velvet, gray, 2 1/3yds (180-200cm) (#2000, 1in (24mm) col. 5)

Looped Flower.......Crepe Georgette, gray, 1yd (100cm) (#4546, 5/8in (15mm) col. 5)

Ribbon for stitching ..Embroidery, purple, 7 2/3yds (700cm) (#1540, 1/8in (3.5mm) col. 198)

Ribbon for embroidery........................
     Embroidery, 4 1/2yds (400cm) (#1540, 1/8in (3.5mm) col. 175) 1 2/3yds (150c
     (#1540, col. 287)

Flowers attached to shoulder strap......
     Single-Face Satin (#1150, 1in (25mm) col. 5 and col. 48) 18in (46cm) each

Other .... Matching #5 Pearl Cotton and embroidery thread, 1 skein each, quilt batting 9
     x 18in (23cm x 46cm), matching fabric for lining 9in x 18in (25cm x 45cm)

Assembly Diagram

1. Cut ribbon (a) into 3in (7.5cm) lengths and place in the center of the quilt batting.

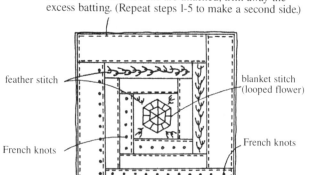

2. For the first row, cut Ribbons (b) and (c) into 4 1/2in (11cm) lengths. Placing them around Ribbon (a), clockwise, stitch into place.

Tuck the last one behind the first and stitch.

5. When all the ribbons are attached, trim away the excess batting. (Repeat steps 1-5 to make a second side.)

feather stitch

blanket stitch (looped flower)

French knots

French knots

6. Embroider the front side only.

7. Put the facing ribbon along the edge of the opening of the bag and sew together, whipstitch from the front side.

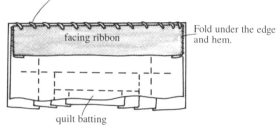

facing ribbon

Fold under the edge and hem.

quilt batting

Instructions for Bag on Page 21 Finished Size: 8 1/4in (21cm) x 8 1/4in (21cm) with 3/4in (2cm) gusset

◆ Materials

Foundation ....All ribbon is Double-Faced Velveteen (#4643)

(a) powder pink	6in (15cm) (3in (75mm) col. 91)
(b) beige	18in (44cm) (1in (25mm) col.10)
(c) peach frost	18in (44cm) (1in (25mm) col. 13)
(d) celery	24in (60cm) (1in (25mm) col. 72)
(e) saffron	24in (60cm) (1in (25mm) col. 15)
(f) celery	1yd (80cm) (1 1/2in (36mm) col. 72)
(g) saffron	1yd (80cm) (1 1/2in (36mm) col. 15)

Facing for opening.......Picot Edge Velvet, beige, 1/2yd (46cm) (#2000, 1in (24mm) col. 11)

Gusset and shoulder strap ..Picot Edge Velvet, beige, 2 1/3yds (200cm) (#2000, 1in (24mm) col. 11)

Looped Flower.............Crepe Georgette, lt peach, 1yd (100cm) (#4546, 5/8in (15mm) col. 64)

Ribbon for stitching ....Embroidery, pink, 7 2/3yds (700cm), (#1540, 1/8in (3.5mm) col. 102)

Ribbon for embroidery ..Embroidery, 2 1/3yds (200cm) each of (#1540, 1/8in (3.5mm) col. 034
and col. 374), 60in (150cm) of #1540, col. 102

Flowers attached to shoulder strap............

Single-Face Satin (#1150, 1in (25mm) col. 10 and col. 15) 1/2yd (46cm) each

Other ....#5 Pearl Cotton and embroidery thread, 1 skein each, quilt batting 9in x 18in
(23cm x 46cm), matching fabric for lining, 9in x 18in (25 x 45cm)

Instructions for sewing foundation ribbons together

Overlap the edges of the ribbons approximately 1/16in (3mm) and stitch down, passing the needle through the quilt batting as you stitch.

3. For the second row, cut ribbon into 6in (15cm) lengths, place on batting in the same manner as the first row and stitch in place.

4. For the third row, cut ribbon into 8in (20cm) lengths, place on batting and stitch into place in the same manner as the first row, leaving 3/8in (1cm) of ribbon around the outside corners to fold under.

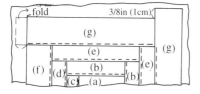

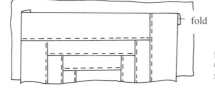

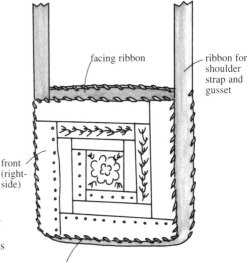

8. Whipstitch shoulder strap ribbon around the edges of the bag to create a gusset.

9. Fold lining in half.

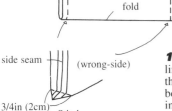

11. Adjust the length of the shoulder strap ribbon, sew the ends together, cover seam with excess ribbon and secure.

10. Place the lining inside the facing ribbon and hem in place.

Place lining 5/8in (1.5cm) lower

12. Make two flowers and attach to the shoulder strap.

Gathered Flower (square) 6in (15cm)

Gathered Flower (hexagon) 12in (31cm)
*Use Template C on page 38.

Project from Page *16*

Linked Flower Hat Band

◆ Materials

Flowers............Single-Face Satin (two pieces), 12in (31cm) of each color (#1150, 1in (25mm) col. 48, 11, 4, 5)

Ribbon for threading flowers...........
Single-Face Satin, lt brown, 1 1/2yd (140cm) (#1150, 5/8in (15mm) col. 48)

Other ....Matching embroidery thread

◆ Assembly Notes: Make two Gathered Flowers (hexagon, Template C on page 38) of each color of ribbon. Thread flower 5/8in (15mm) on satin ribbon and sew each flower into place with one stitch. Be sure to hide the seams on the flowers when arranging them along the ribbon.

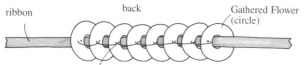

ribbon   back   Gathered Flower (circle)

Thread the ribbon through the eight flowers and sew each into place with one stitch on the back side of the ribbon.

Project from Page *17*

Peony Hat Ornament

◆ Instructions for Flower A

1	Gathered Flower (square)	Pleated Crepe (4647)	1 1/2in (38mm)	antique rose (29)	8in (21cm)
2	Gathered Flower (alternating hexagon)	Pleated Crepe (4647)	1 1/2in (38mm)	antique rose (29)	22in (54cm)

Use Template A (hexagon) on page 38 for Gathered Flower in Ribbon **2**.

◆ Instructions for Flower B

1	Gathered Flower (square)	Pleated Crepe (4647)	1 1/2in (38mm)	gray (5)	8in (21cm)
2	Gathered Flower (alternating hexagon)	Pleated Crepe (4647)	1 1/2in (38mm)	gray (5)	18in (44cm)

Use Template B (hexagon) on page 38 for Gathered Flower in Ribbon **2**.

◆ Instructions for Flower C

1	Gathered Flower (square)	Pleated Crepe (4647)	2in (50mm)	dk mauve (92)	12in (29cm)
2	Gathered Flower (alternating hexagon)	Pleated Crepe (4647)	2in (50mm)	dk mauve (92)	24in (61cm)

Use Template A (hexagon) on page 38 for Gathered Flower in Ribbon **2**.
Other: matching embroidery thread

◆ Assembly Notes: Follow the same instructions to make different colored flowers in small, medium and large sizes, then sew in place on the hat.

Project from Page *22*

Elegant Wine Hat Ornament

◆ Materials

Ribbon ....Stripe Velvet, red, 1 2/3yds (160cm) (#4844, 1 1/2in (38mm) col. 28)

Other................Matching #5 Pearl Cotton

◆ Assembly Notes: Cut the ribbon into lengths of 32in (80cm), 10in (25cm), and 22in (55cm). Following the diagram, make one square and one alternating hexagon Gathered Flower, tie a single knot in the remaining ribbon and thread it through the flowers. With flowers attached, wrap the ribbon around the hat and stitch the ends together.

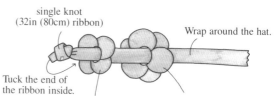

single knot (32in (80cm) ribbon)   Wrap around the hat.

Tuck the end of the ribbon inside.

Gathered Flower (square) (10in (25cm) ribbon)

Gathered Flower (alternating hexagon) (Template A) (22in (55cm) ribbon)

Open center to 3/8in (1cm) diameter.

Open center to 1 1/4in (3cm) diameter.

Project from Page *23*

Velvet Rose Hat Band

1	Single Knot	Single-Face Satin (1150)	3/8in (9mm)	raspberry (98)	4in (10cm)
2	Gathered Flower with two ribbons (circle)	Rayon Satin (1000)	5/8in (15mm)	fuchsia (53)	6 1/2in (17cm)
		Rayon Satin (1000)	1in (25mm)	eggplant (26)	6 1/2in (17cm)
3	Gathered Flower (square)	Bright Velvet (4480)	2in (50mm)	fuchsia (53)	13 1/4in (34cm)
4	Gathered Flower (alternating hexagon)	Bright Velvet (4480)	2in (50mm)	fuchsia (53)	23in (58cm)

Other: ribbon to wrap around hat, Bright Velvet, fuchsia, 1 1/4yd (110cm) (#4480, 1in (25mm) col. 53), matching #5 Pearl Cotton

◆ Assembly Notes: Wrap ribbon around the hat and tie in a soft bow. Fold under ribbon ends to form second loops and stitch in place. Attach the assembled flowers on top of the ribbon.

Accessories in Rich Colors

Instructions for Flower A on Page 24

1	Single Knot	Picot Edge Satin (1600)	5/8in (15mm)	taupe (11)	4 3/4in (12cm)
2	Gathered Flower (pentagon)	Picot Edge Satin (1600)	1in (25mm)	beige (10)	12 1/2in (32cm)
3	Gathered Flower (alternating hexagon)	Velvet (2500)	2in (50mm)	navy (55)	24in (60cm)
4	Gathered Flower (alternating hexagon)	Bright Velvet (4480)	3in (75mm)	rose (29)	1yd (90cm)

Other: matching #5 Pearl Cotton, felt (black) 2 3/4in x 2 3/4in (7cm x 7cm)

◆ **Assembly Notes:** Use Template B (hexagon) on page 38, enlarged two times, for Flower in Ribbon **4**.

Instructions for Flower B on Page 24

1	Single Knot	Rayon Satin (1000)	5/8in (15mm)	fawn (48)	4 3/4in (12cm)
2	Gathered Flower with two ribbons (circle)	Rayon Satin (1000)	5/8in (15mm)	dusty peach (40)	6in (15cm)
		Pleated Satin (0492)	1in (25mm)	dusty rose (65)	6in (15cm)
3	Folded Flower A	Ruffled Satin (0497)	1in (25mm)	ecru (12)	16in (40cm)
4	Foundation (Bow)	Picot Edge Velvet (2000)	1in (24mm)	navy (19)	20in (50cm)

Other: matching embroidery thread

Instructions for Flower C on Page 24

1	Rolled Rose C	Velvet (2500)	1in (25mm)	violet (54)	16in (40cm)
2	Foundation	Velvet (2500)	1in (25mm)	violet (54)	20in (50cm)

Other: matching embroidery thread

◆ **Assembly Notes:** For Foundation in Ribbon **2**, tie a knot in the ribbon, fold the ends in half, thread through the knot and arrange into a double bow.

Instructions for Flower D on Page 24

1	Single Knot	Double-Faced Velvet (4643)	5/8in (15mm)	mauve (92)	4in (10cm)
2	Gathered Flower (square)	Picot Edge Fancy (4552)	★ 1 3/4in (47mm)	beige (10)	10in (26cm)
3	Gathered Flower (pentagon)	Stripe Organdy (4550)	★ 2in (50mm)	mauve (92)	20in (50cm)
4	Gathered Flower (hexagon)	Bright Velvet (4480)	2in (50mm)	antique rose (29)	24in (60cm)

Other: matching #5 Pearl Cotton, felt (black) 2 1/2in x 2 1/2in (6cm x 6cm)

◆ **Assembly Notes:** Use Template D (pentagon) on page 38, for Flower in Ribbon **3**, and use Template A (hexagon) for Flower in Ribbon **4**.

Instructions for Flower E on Page 25

1	Rolled Rose C	Pleated Velvet (0500)	1in (25mm)	cinnamon (9)	22in (55cm)
2	Gathered Flower (alternating hexagon)	Velvet (2500)	1in (25mm)	navy (19)	24in (60cm)
3	Foundation (tied ribbon)	Pleated Velvet (0500)	1 1/2in (38mm)	cinnamon (9)	26in (65cm)

Other: matching #5 Pearl Cotton

◆ **Assembly Notes:** Use Template A (hexagon) on page 38 for Flower in Ribbon **2**. For Foundation in Ribbon **3**, tie ribbon bow and attach barrette or brooch pin to the back.

Instructions for Flower F on Page 25

1	Folded Rose	Wire Edge (533)	1 1/2in (40mm)	pink (22)	1yd (100cm)
2	Gathered Flower (octagon)	Textured Organdy (4584)	★ 1 1/2in (38mm)	pink (94)	24in (60cm)
3	Gathered Flower (octagon)	Pleat Luminous (4640)	2in (50mm)	purple (4)	26in (65cm)

Other: matching #5 Pearl Cotton, felt (black) 2 1/2in x 2 1/2in (6cm x 6cm), small amount of poly-fiber fill.

◆ **Assembly Notes:** Use Template E (octagon) on page 38 for Flowers in Ribbons **2** and **3**.

Instructions for Flower G on Page 25

1	Single Knot	Single-Face Satin (1150)	3/8in (9mm)	ecru (12)	3in (6cm)
2	Gathered Flower with two ribbons (circle)	Rayon Satin (1000)	5/8in (15mm)	fuchsia (53)	6 1/2in (17cm)
		Ruffled Satin (one sided) (0497)	1in (25mm)	antique rose (29)	6 1/2in (17cm)
3	Folded Flower A	Pleated Satin (0492)	1in (25mm)	fuchsia (53)	20in (50cm)
4	Gathered Flower (hexagon)	Bright Velvet (4480)	2in (50mm)	eggplant (26)	24in (60cm)
5	Ribbon Bows	Embroidery (1100)	★ 1/8in (3.5mm)	(57) (53) (28)	1yd (90cm) each

Other: matching #5 Pearl Cotton, felt (black) 2 1/2in x 2 1/2in (6cm x 6cm)

◆ **Assembly Notes:** For Flower in Ribbon **2**, place both ribbons together and make Gathered Flower (circle). Use Template A (hexagon) on page 38 for Flower in Ribbon **4**. Cut each color of Ribbon Bows in **5** into 18in (45cm) lengths to make six pieces, then tie them together in a bow and attach between Flowers in Ribbons **3** and **4**.

Drawstring Bags

Instructions for Handbag on Page 26 Finished Size: 6in (15cm) wide x 6in (15cm) deep

◆ Materials (excluding flowers)

Foundation (a) ..Rayon Satin, fawn, 13in (34cm)
(#1000, 1 7/8in (48mm) col. 48)

Foundation (b)..Stripe Velvet, dark red, 13in
(34cm) (#4844, 1 1/2in (38mm)
col. 28)

Foundation (c)..Rayon Satin, antique green, 13in
(34cm) (#1000, 1in (25mm) col.
15)

Foundation (d)..Picot Edge Satin, antique green,
13in (34cm) (#1600, 1in (24mm)
col. 15)

Foundation (e)..Rayon Satin, fuchsia, 13in (34cm)
(#1000, 1 7/8in (48mm) col. 53)

Drawstring loops....................
Rayon Satin (6 pieces), fawn, 2in (5cm)
(#1000, 5/8in (15mm) col. 48)

Drawstring........Single-Face Satin (2 pieces), dark red, 26in
(65cm), (#1150, 3/8in (9mm) col. 28)

Ribbon for embroidery...........
Embroidery, 3 1/3yds (300cm) each
(#801, col. 23 and col. 8), 3yds (250cm)
(#1540, col. 146) and (#1505, 1/8in
(4mm) wide, col. 53)

Other.................Matching embroidery thread, matching
fabric for lining, 7in x 12 1/2in (18cm x
32cm)

◆ Flower Assembly and Materials Chart

1	Single Knot	Single-Face Satin (1150)	3/8in (9mm)	lilac (63)	4in (10cm)
2	Gathered Flower with two ribbons (circle)	Rayon Satin (1000)	5/8in (15mm)	fuchsia (53)	6in (15cm)
		Ruffled Satin (one sided) (0497)	1in (25mm)	lilac (63)	6in (15cm)

Other: matching #5 Pearl Cotton

Assembly Diagram

6. Fold 3/8in (0.8cm) inside along the top e
of the bag, place the six drawstring loops ev
around the opening and stitch in place with t
strands embroide
thread.

6in (15cm)   3/8in (1cm)

foundation (a) (wrong-side)

fold (b)

(c)

(d)

(e)

5. Fold in half with right-sides together and stitch. Press the seam open.

(right-s

Fold 2in (5cm) length of ribbon in half.

7. Baste around the bottom and gather.

8. Sew the lining same as outside.

6in (15cm)

wrong-side of fabric (back)

7in (18cm)

Baste around the bottom and gather.

9. Wrong sides together, place lining inside bag below top edge and hem in place.

12. Thread the other ribbon from the opposite side and tie.

11. Thread the ribbon for the drawstring through the loops and tie in a knot.

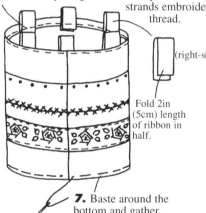

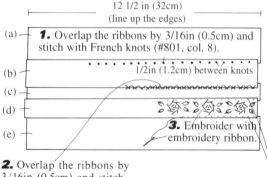

12 1/2 in (32cm) (line up the edges)

(a)

1. Overlap the ribbons by 3/16in (0.5cm) and stitch with French knots (#801, col. 8).

(b)

1/2in (1.2cm) between knots

(c)

(d)

(e)

3. Embroider with embroidery ribbon.

2. Overlap the ribbons by 3/16in (0.5cm) and stitch with herringbone stitch with three strands of embroidery thread.

4. Overlap the ribbons by 1/16in (0.2cm) and stitch together with two strands embroidery thread.

10. Sew assembled flower to the bottom.

French knots and rose (#1540, col. 146)

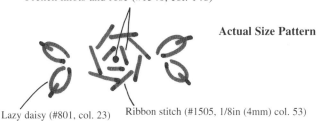

Actual Size Pattern

Lazy daisy (#801, col. 23)   Ribbon stitch (#1505, 1/8in (4mm) col. 53)

Instructions for Bag on Page 27 Finished Size: 5 1/2in (14cm) wide x 5 1/2in (14cm) deep

◆ Materials (excluding flowers)

Foundation (a)....Rayon Satin, antique rose,
12 1/2in (32cm) (#1000, 2in
(48mm) col. 29)

Foundation (b)....Rayon Satin, olive drab,
12 1/2in (32cm) (#1000, 1in
(25mm) col. 43)

Foundation (c)....Rayon Satin, fuchsia, 12 1/2in
(32cm) (#1000, 1in (25mm)
col. 53)

Foundation (d)....Check Velvet, fuchsia, 12 1/2in
(32cm) (#4524, 1in (24mm)
col. 53)

Foundation (e)....Rayon Satin, eggplant, 12 1/2in
(32cm) (#1000, 2in (48mm)
col. 26)

Drawstring loops.............

Rayon Satin (6 pieces), antique
rose, 2in (5cm) (#1000,
5/8in (15mm) col. 29)

Drawstring..........Single-Face Satin (2 pieces)
lilac, 26in (65cm) (#1150,
3/8in (9mm) col. 63)

Ribbon for embroidery...........

Embroidery, #1540, 3yds
(250cm) each of cols. 158,
364 and 160. 3yds (250cm)
#801, col. 8

Other...................Matching embroidery thread,
matching fabric for lining
7in x 12in (17cm x 30cm)

◆ Flower Assembly and Materials Chart

1	Single Knot	Single-Face Satin (1150)	3/8in (9mm)	lilac (63)	4in (10cm)
2	Gathered Flower with two ribbons (circle)	Rayon Satin (1000)	5/8in (15mm)	antique rose (29)	6in (15cm)
		Ruffled Satin (one sided) (0497)	1in (25mm)	lilac (63)	6in (15cm)

Other: matching #5 Pearl Cotton

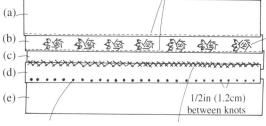

12in (30cm)
(line up the edges)

2. Overlap the ribbons by 1/16in (2mm) and stitch with two strands of embroidery thread.

(a)

(b)

1. Embroider with ribbon.

(c)

(d)

(e)

1/2in (1.2cm) between knots

4. Overlap the ribbons by 3/16in (0.5cm) and stitch with French knots (#1540, 1/8in (3.5mm) col. 160).

3. Overlap the ribbons by 3/16in (0.5cm) and stitch with herringbone stitch with three strands of embroidery thread.

*From this point assemble the bag in the same way as the bag on page 26.

French knots and rose (#1540, 1/8in (3.5mm) col. 158)

Actual Size Pattern

ribbon stitch (#801, col. 8)

lazy daisy (#1540, 1/8in (3.5mm) col. 364)

73

Linked Flower Purses

Instructions for Purse on Page 28 Finished Size: 6in (15cm) wide x 7 1/2in (19cm) deep

◆ Materials

Foundation ......Single-Face Satin, dk olive, 18in (46cm) (#1150, 6in (15cm) col. 16)

Ribbon for threading flowers...........
Single-Face Satin, raspberry, 28in (70cm) (#1150, 3/8in (9mm) col. 98)

Shoulder strap .Fashion cord, purple, 1 1/3yds (120cm) (#90, col. 57)

Ribbon for stitching ....
Embroidery, lt brown, 2yds (200cm) (#1540, 1/8in (3.5mm) col. 480)

Flowers............Pleated Satin, 6in (15cm) each of (#0492, 1in (25mm) col. 53 and col. 99)
Rayon Satin (3 pieces), 6in (15cm) (#1000, 5/8in (15mm) col. 53)
Ruffled Satin (one-sided), 6in (15cm), (#0497, 1in (25mm) col. 63)

Other ....Matching embroidery thread, matching fabric for lining 14in x 7in (35cm x 17cm)

1. Fold the Foundation ribbon in half with right-sides together and stitch a triangle at the bottom.

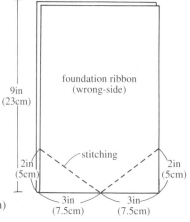

9in (23cm)

foundation ribbon (wrong-side)

stitching

2in (5cm)   2in (5cm)

3in (7.5cm)   3in (7.5cm)

2. Turn right-side out and whipstitch both sides with embroidery ribbon.

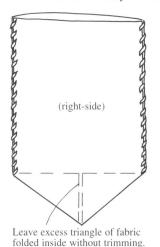

(right-side)

Leave excess triangle of fabric folded inside without trimming.

3. Make three Gathered Flowers (circle), thread together with ribbon, and secure to the ribbon with one stitch on the back side.

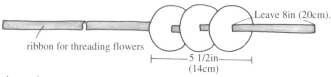

ribbon for threading flowers

Leave 8in (20cm).

5 1/2in (14cm)

4. Fold in 1 5/8in (4cm) along opening edge and attach the strap.

Stitch strap in corners.

1 5/8in (4cm)

1 5/8in (4cm)

(wrong-side)

side seam

(right-side)

5. Wrap the long end of the ribbon around the back of the purse and tie in a bow at the front. Stitch into place on the Foundation.

6. Make the inside lining.

6in (15cm)

7in (17.5cm)

stitch

wrong-side (back)

3/8in (1cm)

3/8in (1cm)

trim

7. Place lining wrong sides together inside bag and hem.

3/4 to 1 1/4in (2-3cm) below edge

inside lining (wrong-side)

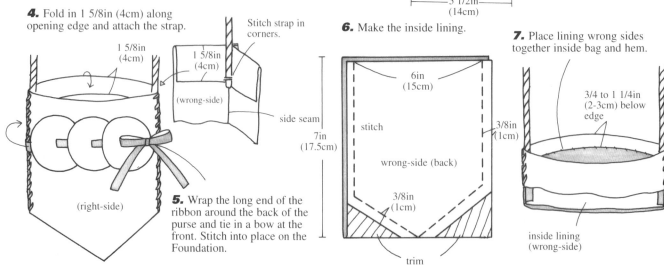

Assembly Diagram

Instructions for Purse on Page 29 Finished Size: 6in (15cm) wide x 7 1/2in (19cm) deep

Attaching the Decorative Ribbons

◆ Materials

Foundation ....Single-Face Satin, dark olive, 18in (46cm) (#1150, 6in (150mm) col. 16)

Decorative ribbon...............
> Pleated Satin, fuchsia, 17in (43cm) (#0492, 1in (25mm) col. 53)

Shoulder strap...Fashion cord, purple, 1 1/3yds (120cm) (#90, col. 57)

Ribbon for stitching ....
> Embroidery, lt brown, 2yds (200cm) (#1540, 1/8in (3.5mm) col. 480)

Flowers ....Rayon Satin, 12in (31cm) each of (#1000, 1in (25mm) col. 53 and col. 26)

Other ....Matching embroidery thread, matching fabric for lining 14in x 7in (35cm x 17cm)

◆ Assembly Notes:
Except for the Decorative ribbon, follow directions for bag on page 28. Use Template C (hexagon) on page 38 for the Flowers, gathering up basting stitches to leave a 1in (2.5cm) hole in the center.

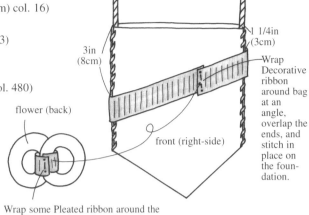

1 1/4in (3cm)

3in (8cm)

Wrap Decorative ribbon around bag at an angle, overlap the ends, and stitch in place on the foundation.

flower (back)

front (right-side)

Wrap some Pleated ribbon around the two flowers and attach to the main Pleated ribbon, hiding the seams.

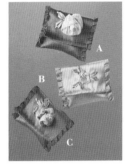

Projects from Page *29*

Small Pouches

Instructions for Small Pouches on Page 29 Finished Size: 2 3/4in (7.2cm) wide x 2 1/4in (5.5cm) deep

◆ Materials for A
Ruffled Satin, dark olive, 7in (17.5cm) (#4895, 2 3/4in (72mm) col. 16), French, pink, 6in (15cm) (#58937, col. 6), Embroidery, green, 20in (50cm) (#1540, 1/4in (7mm) col. 374), matching embroidery thread, one small snap

◆ Materials for B
Ruffled Satin, antique rose, 7in (17.5cm) (#4895, 2 3/4in (72mm) col. 29) Embroidery, ombre, 20in (50cm) each of (#801, col. 8) and (#1540, 1/8in (4mm) col. 4), green, 1yd (100cm) (#801, col. 23), matching embroidery thread, one small snap

◆ Materials for C
Ruffled Satin, blue, 7in (17.5cm) (#4895, 2 3/4in (72mm) col. 46) French, red, 6in (15cm) (#58937, col. 18) Embroidery, green, 20in (50cm) (#1540, 1/4in (7mm) col. 366) matching embroidery thread, one small snap

Actual Size Pattern for A & C

lazy daisy (#1540)

Rolled Rose A (#58937)

Actual Size Pattern for B

lazy daisy (#801, col. 23)

French knots (#1540)

ribbon stitch outside (#801, col. 8)

ribbon stitch inside (#1540)

1. Fold under raw edges of ribbon twice and hem.

flap

2 1/4in (5.5cm)

Ruffled Satin ribbon (wrong-side)

2. Fold.

bottom

2 1/4in (5.5cm)

hem

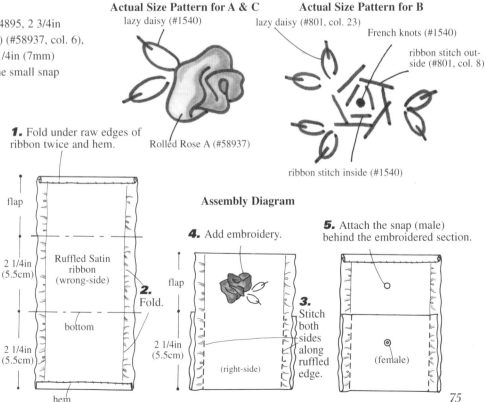

flap

Assembly Diagram

4. Add embroidery.

5. Attach the snap (male) behind the embroidered section.

3. Stitch both sides along ruffled edge.

(right-side)

2 1/4in (5.5cm)

(female)

Wedding Bouquet

Instructions for Bouquet

◆ Materials

Flowers............Crepe Georgette, ecru,
14yds (1,225cm) (#4546,
1in (25mm) col. 12)

Leaves ....Organdy, green (#4563,
1 1/2in (38mm) 1 1/2yds
(140cm) of col. 3, 4 2/3yds
(420cm) of col. 13

Ribbon Bows ..Single-Face Satin, ecru, 2yds
(180cm) (#1150, 1 1/2in
(36mm) col. 12) Pleated
Satin, ecru, 1 1/4yds (110cm)
(#0492, 5/8in (15mm) col.
12)

Other ....Matching embroidery thread,
approximately 80 florist
wires (#30), one roll of florist
tape (green), small amount of
double-sided tape

Instructions for Flowers for Gloves

◆ Materials

Flowers............Crepe Georgette, ecru, 2yds
(154cm) (#4546, 5/8in
(15mm) col. 12)
Single-Face Satin, ecru, 13in
(34cm) (#1150, 1in (25mm)
col. 12)

Other ....Matching embroidery thread

◆ Assembly Procedure

1. Cut Crepe Georgette ribbon into six 8in
(20cm) pieces and make six of Rolled Rose B.
Cut the remaining 13in (34cm) of ribbon into
two 7in (17cm) pieces and set aside (for
Gathered Flowers).

2. Cut Single-Face Satin ribbon into two 6in
(17cm) pieces, place each together with a
piece of the Crepe Georgette and make two
Gathered Flowers (circle).

3. Arrange three of the Rolled Rose B flowers
in the center of each Gathered Flower and
secure in place.

4. Attach to the gloves.

◆ Assembly Notes

Use 14in (35cm) of ribbon for each flower. Make about 35 of Rolled Rose B. Use 5 1/2in
(14cm) of ribbon for each leaf. Make 10 of Leaf A using col. 3 ribbon, and about 30 using
col. 13 ribbon.

Assembly Diagram

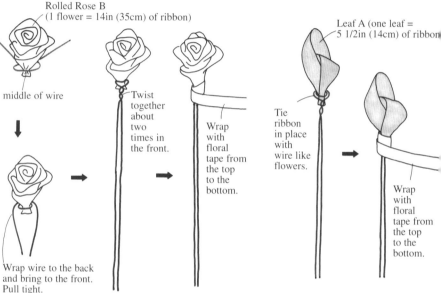

Rolled Rose B
(1 flower = 14in (35cm) of ribbon)

Leaf A (one leaf =
5 1/2in (14cm) of ribbon)

middle of wire

Twist together about two times in the front.

Wrap with floral tape from the top to the bottom.

Tie ribbon in place with wire like flowers.

Wrap with floral tape from the top to the bottom.

Wrap wire to the back and bring to the front. Pull tight.

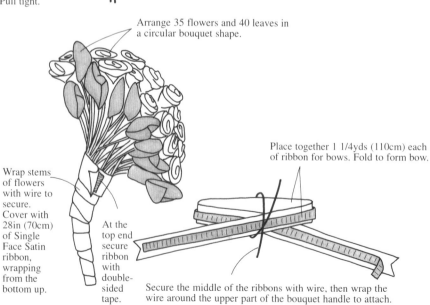

Arrange 35 flowers and 40 leaves in a circular bouquet shape.

Wrap stems of flowers with wire to secure. Cover with 28in (70cm) of Single Face Satin ribbon, wrapping from the bottom up.

At the top end secure ribbon with double-sided tape.

Place together 1 1/4yds (110cm) each of ribbon for bows. Fold to form bow.

Secure the middle of the ribbons with wire, then wrap the wire around the upper part of the bouquet handle to attach.

Black Satin Evening Bag

Instructions for Evening Bag
Finished Size: 8in (20cm) wide x 8 1/2in (22cm) deep, with 2 1/2in (6.5cm) gusset

◆ Materials (excluding flowers)

Foundation ......Ruffled Satin (one-sided),
black, 22in (56cm) (#0497,
6in (150mm) col. 3)

Shoulder strap .Picot Edge Satin, black,
1 1/3yds (120cm) (#1600,
5/8in (15mm) col. 3)

Other ....One skein #5
Pearl Cotton,
fabric for lin-
ing (black),
20in x 12in
(50cm x 30cm),
one large black snap

◆ Flower Assembly and Materials Chart

1	Rolled Rose C	Suede Tape (2200)	1 3/8in (35mm)	cocoa (47)	26in (65cm)
2	Gathered Flower (alternating hexagon)	Taffeta (4495)	2in (50mm)	fawn (48)	24in (60cm)

◆ Assembly Notes: Use Template A (hexagon) on page 38 for Gathered Flower in Ribbon **2**.

1. Cut Ruffled Satin ribbon in two 11in (28cm) pieces.

5 1/2in (14cm)
1/4in (6mm) seam

(wrong-side)

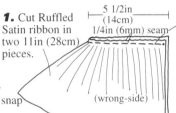

2. Fold in half with right-sides together and stitch along the ruffled side.

* Follow these steps to make a second side.

3. Match the sides with right-sides together and stitch around the outside. Turn right side out.

1/4in (6mm) from edge of ribbon

(wrong-side)

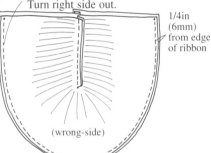

4. Fold ribbon inside along the opening edge and hem in place.

3/4in (2cm)

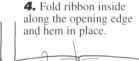

6. Attach ribbon for strap to both sides.

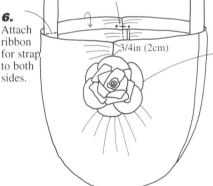

5. Stitch flower tightly in place over the front seam.

7. Make the lining.

11in (28cm)

10in (25cm)

lining (wrong-side)

3/8in (1cm)

Stitch a curve at the bottom.

Trim

Assembly Diagram

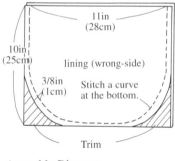

8. Place the lining inside bag wrong-sides together and hem.

3/8in (1cm) below edge

inside lining (wrong-side)

9. Attach snap.

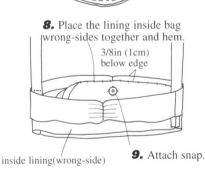

10. Create gusset.

ribbon for strap

1in (2.5cm) 1in (2.5cm)

pleat side seam

To make gusset, pleat 1in (2.5cm) together and stitch in place.

1in (2.5cm)

1in (2.5cm)

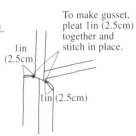

Instructions for Red Flower

◆ Flower Assembly and Materials Chart

1	Rolled Rose C	Velvet (2500)	1in (25mm)	red (1)	24in (60cm)
2	Foundation (tied bow)	Pleated Velvet (0500)	1in (25mm)	dk brown (7)	20in (50cm)

Other: matching embroidery thread, felt (black) 2in x 2in (5cm x 5cm)

◆ Assembly Notes: Tie the Foundation ribbon in Ribbon **2** in a bow and attach to the back of Flower in Ribbon **1**.

Embroidered Rose Pouches

◆ Materials for A

Ruffled Satin, antique green, 8 1/4in (21cm) (#4996, col. 15), Embroidery (#1540, 1/8in (3.5mm) col. 424 and col. 445) 1yd (100cm) each, (#1100, 1/4in (5mm) col. 32 and col. 60), 20in (50cm) each, (#801, col. 23) 1yd (100cm), matching embroidery thread

◆ Materials for B (Eyeglasses holder)

Double Faced Velvet, dusty rose (#4643, col. 65) 16 1/2in (42cm) of 3in (75mm) and 14in (35cm) of 5/8in (15mm), Embroidery (#1540, 1/4in (7mm) col. 63) 1yd (100cm), (#1540, 1/8in (3.5mm) col. 74) 2yds (200cm), (#801, col. 15) 1 2/3yds (150cm), (#1505, 3/8in (8mm) col. 40) 1yd (100cm),
Fashion cord (#90, col. 40) 24in (60cm), matching embroidery thread

◆ Materials for C (Eyeglasses holder)

Double Faced Velvet (#4643, col. 13) 17in (42cm) of 3in (75mm) and 14in (35cm) of 5/8in (15mm), Embroidery (#1540, 1/4in (7mm) col. 112) 1yd (100cm), (#1505, 3/8in (8mm) col. 40) 1yd (100cm), (#801, col. 15) 1 2/3yds (150cm), (#1540, 1/8in (3.5mm) col. 23) 2yds (200cm), Fashion cord (#90, col. 59) 24in (60cm), matching embroidery thread

◆ Materials for D

Silk Moiré, pale pink, 10in (25cm) (#20001, 4in (10cm) col. 31), Crepe Georgette, ecru, 1yd (100cm) (#4546, 5/8in (15mm) col. 12), Embroidery (#1100, 1/8in (3.5mm)) 2yds (200cm) of col. 17, 1 2/3yds (150cm) of col. 63, (#1540, 1/8in (3.5mm) col. 374) 1yd (100cm), matching #5 Pearl Cotton

◆ Materials for E

Ruffled Satin, ecru, 8 1/4in (21cm) (#4996, col. 12), Embroidery (#1540, 1/8in (3.5mm) col. 143 and col. 163) 1yd (100cm) each, (#1100, 1/4in (5mm) col. 63) 1yd (100cm), (#801, col. 23) 1yd (100cm), matching embroidery thread

◆ Materials for F

Ruffled Edge Satin, beige, 8 1/2in (22cm) (#4895, 2 3/4in (72mm) col. 10), Single-Face Satin, taupe, 5 1/2in (14cm) (#1150, 3/8in (9mm) col. 11), Embroidery (#1540, 1/8in (3.5mm) col. 63, col. 374) 1yd (100cm) each, (#1540, col. 9) 20in (50cm) (#1100, 1/4in (5mm) col. 40) 1yd (100cm), matching embroidery thread

◆ Materials for G

Ruffled Edge Satin, dusty peach, 8 1/2in (22cm) (#4895, 2 3/4in (72mm) col. 40), Single-Face Satin, dusty rose, 5 1/2in (14cm) (#1150, 3/8in (9mm) col. 65), Embroidery (#1540, 1/8in (3.5mm) col. 102, col. 366) 1yd (100cm) each, (#1100, 1/4in (5mm) col. 00, col. 40, col. 29) 20in (50cm) each, matching embroidery thread

◆ Materials for H

Ruffled Satin, pale pink, 8 1/4in (21cm) (#4996, col. 31), Embroidery (#1540, 1/8in (3.5mm) col. 4 and col. 52) 1yd (100cm) each, (#1100, 1/4in (5mm) col. 40) 1yd (100cm), matching embroidery thread

◆ Materials for I

Ruffled Satin, apricot, 6 1/2in (17cm) (#4996, col. 63), Embroidery (#1540, col. 102, col. 71) 1yd (100cm) each, (#801, col. 23) 1yd (100cm), matching embroidery thread

◆ Materials for J

Picot Taffeta, pink, 7 3/4in (20cm) (#4522, 2 1/4in (52mm) col. 40, Embroidery (#1540, col. 71, col. 143, col. 74) 1yd (100cm) each, (#801, col. 23) 1yd (100cm), matching embroidery thread

◆ Materials for K

Silk Moiré, beige, 10in (25cm) (#20001, 4in (10cm) col. 10), Crepe Georgette, lt peach, 1yd (100cm) (#4546, 5/8in (15mm) col. 64), Embroidery (#1540, 1/8in (3.5mm)) 2yds (200cm) of col. 468, 1 2/3yds (150cm) of col. 37, (#1100, 1/4in (5mm) col. 49) 1yd (100cm), matching #5 Pearl Cotton

**Pattern for A, E, H
(half of actual size)**

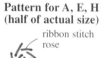

ribbon stitch rose

lazy daisy

**Pattern for B, C
(half of actual size)**

ribbon stitch rose

lazy daisy

French knots

**Pattern for D, K
(half of actual size)**

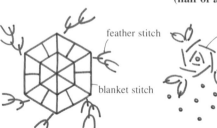

feather stitch

blanket stitch

**Pattern for F, G
(half of actual size)**

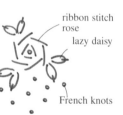

ribbon stitch rose

lazy daisy

French knots

**Pattern for I
(half of actual)**

ribbon rose

lazy daisy

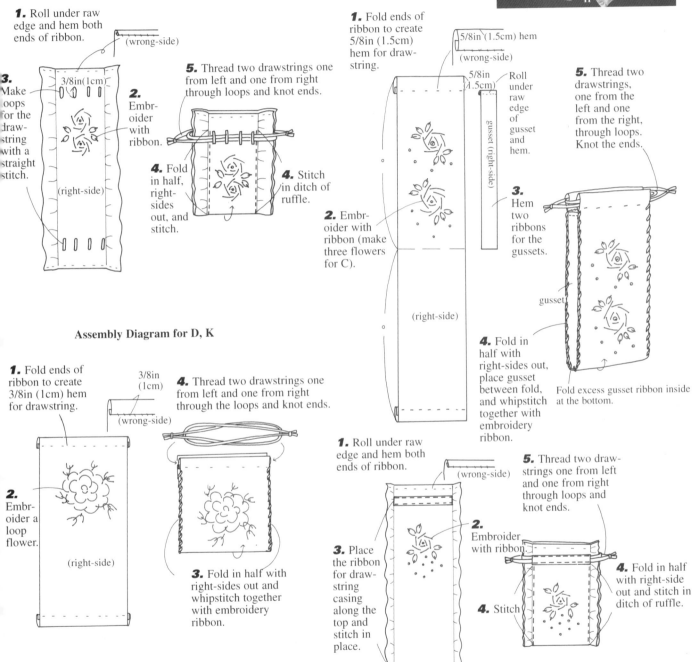

Assembly Diagram for A, E, H, I, J

1. Roll under raw edge and hem both ends of ribbon.

(wrong-side)

3/8in(1cm)

3. Make loops for the drawstring with a straight stitch.

(right-side)

2. Embroider with ribbon.

5. Thread two drawstrings one from left and one from right through loops and knot ends.

4. Fold in half, right-sides out, and stitch.

4. Stitch in ditch of ruffle.

Assembly Diagram for B, C

1. Fold ends of ribbon to create 5/8in (1.5cm) hem for drawstring.

5/8in (1.5cm) hem

(wrong-side)

5/8in (1.5cm)

Roll under raw edge of gusset and hem.

gusset (right-side)

2. Embroider with ribbon (make three flowers for C).

(right-side)

3. Hem two ribbons for the gussets.

5. Thread two drawstrings, one from the left and one from the right, through loops. Knot the ends.

gusset

4. Fold in half with right-sides out, place gusset between fold, and whipstitch together with embroidery ribbon.

Fold excess gusset ribbon inside at the bottom.

Assembly Diagram for D, K

1. Fold ends of ribbon to create 3/8in (1cm) hem for drawstring.

3/8in (1cm)

(wrong-side)

4. Thread two drawstrings one from left and one from right through the loops and knot ends.

2. Embroider a loop flower.

(right-side)

3. Fold in half with right-sides out and whipstitch together with embroidery ribbon.

1. Roll under raw edge and hem both ends of ribbon.

(wrong-side)

3. Place the ribbon for drawstring casing along the top and stitch in place.

2. Embroider with ribbon.

5. Thread two drawstrings one from left and one from right through loops and knot ends.

4. Stitch

4. Fold in half with right-side out and stitch in ditch of ruffle.

Assembly Diagram for F, G

(wrong-side)

Fold ends of ribbon for drawstring casing and hem.

79

NEEDLEWORK ARTIST YUKIKO OGURA was born in Aichi Prefecture, Japan and attended Kuwasawa Design School, where she studied Basic Interior Design and Fashion Design. Upon graduating, she first designed children's clothing and later contributed needlework and embroidery projects to Japanese books and magazines. She has a reputation for elegant patterns, clear techniques, and original ideas. All the projects in this book are her creations.

Ms. Ogura's unique artistry goes beyond the realm of craft, as her series of fabric and thread collages "Arabian Nnights" and her collaborative creations with French needlework artist Fanny Viollet demonstrate. Their work together develops through an organic process with each artist contributing to the piece and returning it to the other until it is completed.

Ms. Ogura participates in many exhibitions, both overseas and in Japan, including the Worldwide Needlework Exhibition. Her work with Fanny Viollet has been exhibited in both France and Japan. She has written many other books including *Bead Embroidery* (Gakken), *New Embroidery* (Shufu no Tomosha), *Dye-stitch Work Embroidery*, *Bead Embroidery Presents* (Boutique-sha), *Dye-stitch Work Book*, *Fleur d'Amour Work* (Shufu to Seikatsusha), *Line Stitch Work* (Bunka Shuppankyoku), and *Ribbon Embroidery* (Nihon Vogue-sha).